Thinking allowed?

"If journalism is the first draft of history, it is best to get a draft that doesn't miss the wood for the trees. A diligent mind is at work in these essays."

—Janadas Devan, Senior Writer and Columnist,
The Straits Times

Wishing you good health
and happy days,

From us at S2.
2007.

Thinking allowed?

politics, fear and change in Singapore

Warren Fernandez

with cartoons by Miel

SNP•EDITIONS

an imprint of

SNP•INTERNATIONAL

This book includes 27 articles previously published in
The Straits Times.

Published by SNP International
a division of SNP Media Asia Pte Ltd
491 River Valley Road
#01-19/20 Valley Point
Singapore 248371
Tel: (65) 6733 6163   Fax: (65) 6733 3671
snpinternational@snpcorp.com
http://www.snpcorp.com

TEAM SNP
Shirley Hew, Publisher
Shova Loh, Publishing Manager
Tuck Loong, Creative Director
Clara Wong, Marketing & Operations Manager

Printed in Singapore

National Library Board Singapore Cataloguing in Publication Data

Fernandez, Warren.
        Thinking allowed? : politics, fear and change in Singapore /Warren
Fernandez ; with cartoons by Miel. – Singapore : SNP Editions, c2004.
        p. cm.
        Includes index.
        ISBN : 981-248-061-7

1. Political participation – Singapore. 2. Political planning – Singapore –
Citizen participation. 3. Singapore – Politics and government. I. Title.

JQ1063.A58
320.95957 — dc21   SLS2003037081

To my father,
who encouraged me to think aloud

Contents

Introduction

POLITICAL DEBATE in Singapore is hampered by two major inhibitions. First, many assume that politics simply does not exist. For years, whenever I mentioned to someone that I was a political correspondent for *The Straits Times*, the response was predictable: 'Politics? What politics?'

Yet, even in Singapore, with its dominant one-party system, and the People's Action Party having been in power for more than four decades, politicians do not operate with an absolutely free hand. There are the obvious legal and constitutional constraints, as well as the need to bear in mind international opinion. No doubt, some critics would dismiss this, noting that a party with the overwhelming majority the PAP enjoys can choose to disregard or sidestep these concerns.

Even so, Singapore's leaders know that, ultimately, they have to weigh public sentiment, the prevailing mood, as well as more deep-seated interests and values held by segments of the population, which sometimes conflict with those of other groups.

As a political journalist for over a decade, I have watched these forces at work. It made clear to me, for example, that no government in Singapore could make changes to any education policy that would affect the teaching of the mother tongue without making sure it could carry the Chinese ground with it (see page 146). Or, on the thorny issue of reforming the Central Provident Fund pension system, the government has had to proceed carefully, soft-selling its proposals when earlier ones provoked a public uproar (see page 69). It was significant that, only in August 2003, when its standing with the people was at a high following the decisive way it handled the Sars crisis, did the government decide to embark on the most massive reforms of the CPF system, implementing some of the changes which it had been attempting to make since the 1980s. So, no one should imagine that politicians in Singapore have carte blanche to do as they choose, even if they do have a freer hand than leaders elsewhere. How they go about exercising the considerable power they wield is one of the major themes that I have tried to develop in this book.

The second dampener on debate relates to that other major concern of those who might take part in political discussions – the fear factor or chilling effect that robust responses from some politicians are said to have in deterring citizens from exercising their right to speak up and be engaged in the political process.

As a regular commentator on Singapore politics, I have had to straddle the so-called 'Out of Bounds' or OB markers, a golfing metaphor referring to areas of public debate which are best not ventured into by the fainthearted. It has not stopped me from voicing my views. I have also been directly involved in several of the government's public consultation efforts, from the Cost Review Committee to the Singapore 21 Committee and, most recently, the Remaking Singapore Committee. In all these cases, I have found a willingness to test ideas, stretch arguments, and engage in healthy, even robust debate.

True, some views and comments have sparked sharp responses from some government leaders. This is said to have frightened many into believing that the government would rather that the people simply remain silent and leave it to get on with the job. What makes matters worse is that it is impossible to tell beforehand which of these issues or views is likely to draw flak. They change depending on the prevailing circumstances. One needs to walk into an OB marker and get zapped by the proverbial bolt of lightning to discover that it is there. Herein lies the rub of the OB markers issue, which has dogged political discussion for years now.

Yet, my own experience has led me to conclude that Singaporeans sometimes overplay the 'fear factor'. More often than not, it is not a question of which and what issues can be raised for public debate, but rather a matter of how and when to do so. Provided a criticism is honestly made and backed by convictions, I doubt very much that the sky will come tumbling down on the commentator. Besides, I have always believed that the more Singaporeans spoke up, the more likely it would be that the practice of citizens expressing their views, and grappling with contending opinions in a diverse society, would become entrenched in our evolving political culture.

The converse is certainly true: if Singaporeans allow themselves to believe that political discussion is taboo and shrink from exercising their rights, then the space for such discussions will diminish with time, through lack of practice and unfamiliarity with the need to accommodate a range of interests and views in a complex society. Singaporeans would have only themselves to blame if we allowed this to happen.

This book is my humble attempt to help further the process of engaging Singaporeans in thinking about our collective future. It is an attempt to throw up questions and spark thought, rather than offer a menu of answers, for the simple and honest reason that I don't have all the answers.

The essays are drawn from my columns and editorials in *The Straits Times* over the years, especially Thinking Aloud, My View and From the Gallery. Rereading them, I have found that certain themes recur in Singapore politics: democracy and how it might work in a young society, the rising cost of living and how to contain it, dealing with the stresses and strains of mounting economic competition, preserving the past even as we face the future, keeping our ethnic heritage alive as we foster a new Singaporean ethos, dealing with our prickly neighbours while reaching out to the wider world. All these are issues that Singaporeans have been grappling with over the past decade, and more.

While the columns I wrote were meant to be reflective pieces on the most topical issues of the times, I found myself returning to several issues and themes over and again, shaping my own thoughts along the way. Naturally, some of my views changed with time and maturity, but perhaps what was more surprising was how much remained constant over the years.

To be useful to readers, this book is not simply a compilation of previously published columns. A retrospective work would be of interest only to my close associates and myself. Instead, I have identified major recurring themes in Singapore politics and written fresh essays on these issues to set them in the proper context. These make no pretence of being academic theses. To engage readers, I have kept the essays as brief as possible and close to the conversational style of my newspaper columns. They are backed by a selection of relevant past columns that flesh out the ideas, based on actual events and debates over the years. Taken together, I believe they will give readers interested in the politics of Singapore a sense of some of the issues it has had to grapple with in the recent past, and which will shape its course in the years to come.

As the challenges that will confront us become ever more complex, thinking will not only have to be allowed, but positively encouraged all round, if we are to find answers to some of the pressing questions at hand.

Warren Fernandez
August 2004

Acknowledgments

This book is the brainchild of Shova Loh, my editor at SNP Media Asia, who planted the idea of a compilation of my columns published in *The Straits Times* over the years. She persisted in persuading me that such a book would contribute to political discussion in Singapore. For her patient support and advice, I owe her my thanks.

My gratitude – and love – goes to my dear mother, who painstakingly filed every column I wrote since becoming a journalist in 1990. This assured me that no matter what happened, I would at least have one approving reader for every piece I wrote.

Later, my wife, Sally, would join this cheerful band of supporters. She has made it a point to read just about every one of my columns before it went to print, acting as in-house 'editor-in-chief', giving me many helpful comments to hone my arguments and refine my writing.

I owe a debt also to my editor, Han Fook Kwang, who has overseen my work throughout the years, first as Political Editor and now as Editor of *The Straits Times*. He made clear to me that thinking was certainly allowed and should in no way be constrained, even if at times my ideas or language had to be tempered, tested further or tossed out altogether. He probably did more than anyone to keep me in journalism all these years.

Several of my colleagues and friends at the paper – Sumiko Tan, Asad Latif, Chua Mui Hoong, Janadas Devan – also took the time to offer many suggestions to sharpen and tighten the book. So too did my sister Karen. Arun Mahizhnan, deputy director of the Institute of Policy Studies, kindly read the drafts and offered a quote for use on the cover. *Straits Times* artist Dengcoy Miel gamely took up my request to do a set of new illustrations for the book, and delivered these in double-quick time.

To them, and all who have offered help, advice, support and friendship along the way, thank you.

What next, after 2001 sweep?

To have garnered 75 per cent of the vote and a near clean sweep in the 2001 elections was no mean feat in this day and age, even for the PAP. It raises the question of just how the PAP is going to repeat this victory in 2007, when a new man might be leading the party into the polls. Will failure to do so be seen as a setback? A repudiation of the new team? That would be unfortunate, not least for the blow it will deal to the process of political transition here. Worse, there is the danger that if the PAP gets caught in the numbers game and becomes hell-bent on repeating the feat, it may well end up upping the ante at election time to try to do so. That would be foolhardy. In the absence of a national crisis, no party should regard a clean sweep at the polls as a matter of course, especially in a highly educated and urbanised electorate. Broad as the PAP church might be, there must be room in a democracy for other voices, other views.

(From 'Will a dominant PAP also be domineering?'
10 November 2001, see page 48)

Chapter 1
At home, and afraid?

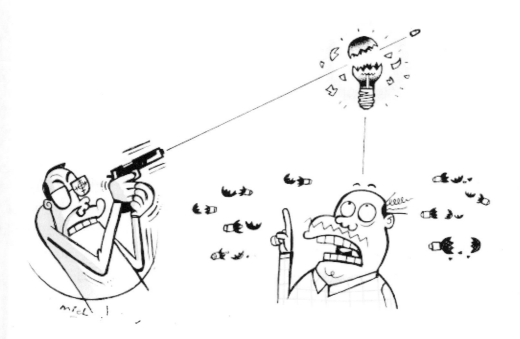

FIGHTING BACK TEARS, Goh Chok Tong declared, 'Your proposals and suggestions will be studied carefully.' He and the audience roared with laughter.

The former prime minister just could not keep a straight face that afternoon. Minutes earlier, he had sat through a skit performed at the Remaking Singapore Committee's report presentation ceremony, held at the Fullerton Hotel. Not wanting a run-of-the-mill, hand-over-the-report session, committee members had commissioned playwright Eleanor Wong, herself a member of the RSC, to write a play that would sum up their months of deliberations. Ms Wong did not disappoint. She poked irreverent fun at both the work of the committee, as well as the government ministers who had appointed it, only to reject some of its ideas, even as these were still being discussed.

'Your proposals and suggestions will be studied carefully,' a character from the play declared, taking a humorous and unvarnished jab at the government's stock answer to 'feedback'.

'We don't go round with air-rifles shooting down ideas!' cried another character, mimicking a line used by some government leaders when asked by reporters why they had been so quick to shoot down some of the committee's proposals.

Mr Goh sat impassively throughout the 15-minute skit, smiling, and laughing at times. When the time came for him to address the audience of young professionals, businessmen, civil servants and civic society members, many must have wondered how he was going to react. Was he going to take issue with this *boh tua boh sueh* (no big, no small, in Hokkien, meaning to show disrespect) taking of liberties?

Not a bit of it. Good-humouredly, he joked that the playwright had preempted his speech, and stolen some of his lines. He struggled to continue. When it came round to the part of his speech where he was to announce that the ideas in the committee's report would be 'studied carefully' and not 'shot down', he simply cracked up. The audience joined him with laughter, and applause. With this prime minister, it seemed, thinking was indeed allowed, even if it was a little cheeky. The fact that Mr Goh recognised the humour in the situation, and was prepared to laugh along, won over his audience.

The scene that afternoon struck me as remarkable, especially in a place like Singapore, where politics is often considered a serious business, for tough-minded men, pursuing farsighted, down-to-earth agendas. People set little store by too much philosophising, dithering with ideologies and emotions, or descending into flippancy and humour. Indeed, after four decades in power, the ruling People's Action Party has come to pride itself on its hard-won reputation for pragmatism and efficacy, not least its willingness to take what it calls 'unpopular but necessary' measures. Ministers are loath to be considered weak, populist, or overly accommodating. In this regard, Mr Goh's willingness to laugh at himself and what some people said about the government was refreshing, even endearing.

For many Singaporeans, politics is for the foolhardy. Talk to Singaporeans, especially younger ones, and you will hear all about their reluctance to speak up on public issues, for fear that voicing their views will land them in the government's 'black book', earmarked for retribution. Others, equally cynical, lament that even if they were not blacklisted, their ideas would simply enter a 'black hole', disappearing unheard into an abyss of previous consultation efforts.

Partly to counter this, the government has launched wave upon wave of committees – Agenda for Action, Singapore 21, Remaking

Singapore – drawing in several thousand people each time into the policy-making and feedback-gathering process. I have had the privilege of being a member of the Singapore 21 and Remaking Singapore committees. In each case, I found the process to be open and uninhibited. People came and spoke their minds, and were encouraged to do so. Most importantly, these were not just cynical exercises in allowing citizens to vent some spleen, but carried out in genuine eagerness to seek and test out new perspectives and ideas. Many of those I know who were involved in these sessions, when ideas were exchanged, views accommodated and compromises reached, were happy that they had chosen to engage and be engaged. Unfortunately, for many others who remained oblivious of the discussions that often took place away from the public eye, these efforts came to be seen as just so much political window dressing. Critics were quick to dismiss the committee reports as propaganda, seizing on examples of ideas and suggestions that are not taken up as more evidence that the government is either not listening, or simply pretending to do so, while having already made up its mind. And so the cycle of cynicism and apathy builds up.

Indeed, when the Remaking Singapore Committee announced in April that most of its recommendations had been taken up or were being considered by the government, the critics changed tack from lamenting that the committee's ideas had been dismissed, to charging that since so many proposals were accepted by the authorities, the committee must have only fought battles it thought it could win. This was ironic, to say the least. But it also said much about the deep – and to my mind, corrosive – cynicism which has set in among some segments of our society.

Lamentably, the idea has taken root among some Singaporeans that politics is taboo, that it's best to keep your thoughts to yourself, disconnect from the process, leave politics to the politicians and get on with paying the mortgage. The PAP's overwhelming majority and its domination of politics, both in and out of Parliament, has left some with a sense that they can do little to change or influence policy. I have encountered this response many times: 'You cover politics? In Singapore? Can't be very much to do?'

Some go further. Because politicians in this country are wont to declare they do not govern by polls or bend with the populist wind, it has become fashionable, in some circles, to scoff at the very idea of democracy as so much liberal pie in the sky. Democracy is associated with inefficiency and ineffectiveness – practised in disorderly and politically rumbunctious places like the Philippines. Until its relatively recent economic takeoff, India was included in this unfortunate category. Too few Singaporeans, I think, view democracy as a precious gift from our forefathers who fought for the right of Singaporeans to choose their own leaders and determine their own future. Many view elections here as being a formality, the outcome a foregone conclusion. That is unfortunate.

Sure, democracy is by no means a panacea for developing societies. It is neither necessary nor sufficient for societal progress. Yet, for all its faults and failings, I believe the liberal democratic system, which we have inherited and adapted along the way, remains the best way for Singaporeans to pick and endorse our leaders. It is also vital for fostering a crucial social compact and collective vision between the people and their leaders on the way forward for our fledgling society.

Singapore's commitment to the rule of law, good governance, openness, accountability and transparency, as well as its deep-seated rejection of corruption, has become part of the fabric of the system and ingrained in its political culture over the years, thanks to the zeal with which the country's founding fathers, led by Lee Kuan Yew, made these the hallmarks of their government. This, thankfully, is Singapore's liberal, democratic heritage. It is something to be celebrated, cherished – and safeguarded.

Besides, even in the narrower field of electoral politics, a quick sweep of recent history will make clear that while the PAP has won every election since 1959, the path to victory has not always been plain sailing. Consider:

❖ 1981: In the Anson by-election, Workers' Party chief J.B. Jeyaretnam broke the PAP's domination of Parliament, edging first past the post with 51.9 per cent of the valid votes. The result took PAP leaders by surprise. Lee Kuan Yew recounts in his memoirs: 'I did not take part in the by-election campaign, leaving it completely to Goh and the younger ministers. They were confident we would win, but when the votes were counted on polling day, we had lost. It was quite a shock...'

❖ 1984: The PAP was hit by a 12-percentage point swing against it. The post-election press conference was a tense affair, with black faces all round the PAP camp. Then Prime Minister Lee wondered aloud about the continued viability of the democratic system, not least since promising new talents whom the PAP had hoped to nurture for Cabinet positions, such as Mah Bow Tan, were among those rejected by the voters.

❖ 1988: Dubbed the 'Eunos election' after the contest in the multi-member ward, called a Group Representation Constituency, caught the popular imagination. An opposition team led by lawyer Francis Seow came close to making history with a first-ever GRC sweep when it won 49.1 per cent of the valid votes at Eunos GRC, after a fierce electoral fight.

❖ 1991: The 'ground is sweet' election, so-called because grassroots leaders had convinced the new Prime Minister Goh that the political ground was solidly behind him after a series of high-profile visits to the constituencies. Held just nine months after Mr Goh took over the premiership from Mr Lee in November 1990, the PAP banked on his popularity as well as his pledge to foster a more consultative style of government. The opposition played its 'joker', invoking its 'by-election strategy', telling voters that they could cast their ballots for the opposition without fear since the PAP would be returned to government with a majority of seats in Parliament on Nomination Day. This was perhaps the greatest backhanded compliment any opposition party anywhere in the world has paid a ruling party. But the strategy worked, and led to opposition candidates sweeping four seats, dislodging an incumbent minister, Dr Seet Ai Mee. Political unknowns such as the Singapore Democratic Party's Cheo Chai Chen and Ling How Doong came from nowhere to defeat heavyweight PAP candidates such as Dr Seet and Ng Pock Too. As a political correspondent for *The Straits Times*, I was at the Conference Hall on election night, August 31, tracking the returns as they came in and watching the shock and horror on many PAP supporters' faces, including that of a crestfallen PM Goh, who took the setback personally.

❖ 1997: The year of the Tang Liang Hong affair. In the run-up to the election, the PAP had focused its firepower on the SDP's new chief, Dr Chee Soon Juan. It sought to defuse thorny issues such as the rising cost of living and high medical costs. But these issues took a back seat when a political wild card emerged from out of the blue, in the form of Mr Tang, whom the PAP dubbed a dangerous 'Chinese chauvinist'. But it was only after the PAP pulled out all the stops, throwing the weight of the prime minister and deputy prime ministers behind the PAP's Cheng San GRC team, that it won narrowly, with 54.8 per cent of the valid votes. It was a bitterly fought campaign, with PAP leaders revealing ominously on the eve of Polling Day that they would be able to track which precincts backed their candidates, with the hint that retribution would follow for those areas that did not vote for them.

❖ 2001: Jobs, jobs, jobs. In the wake of the September 11 terrorist attacks in New York and Washington, PM Goh seized the moment to seek a fresh mandate and political backing for what he said were the tough measures needed to secure Singapore's future in an uncertain world. At stake were jobs, as unemployment was mounting, and the rapid economic growth and high living standards that Singaporeans had grown used to. Again, the PAP was returned to power, taking 65.5 per cent of the seats on Nomination Day. Several political watchers warned Mr Goh not to pin his hopes on securing a larger share of the vote than in previous elections, lest chasing this number forced the PAP to up the political ante during the hustings, or even risk another disappointing setback on Polling Day. A few seats, such Nee Soon East, Chua Chu Kang, Potong

Pasir and Jurong GRC were keenly contested. But in the face of uncertain times, the voters took no chances and plumbed for the tried-and-tested PAP.

The opposition did themselves few favours. The SDP's Dr Chee shot himself in the foot with an outburst against a popular prime minister, demanding that Mr Goh face-off with him before the voters at a public market place. The PAP poured scorn on such thuggish tactics and voters seemed turned off by the SDP, thereby hitting its vote and possibly even that of other opposition parties. On election night, much to everyone's surprise, including many in the PAP, the ruling party enjoyed a massive 10-percentage point gain, reversing much of the 12-percentage point swing against it in 1984. It swept 75.3 per cent of the valid votes cast, a stunning showing that left some wondering how the party would better this performance at the next polls, due by 2007, when a new team would be at the helm and eager to prove it enjoyed strong backing from the voters.

Even this cursory look at recent electoral history should make plain that it would be foolhardy for anyone – whether from the PAP or the opposition – to assume that the outcome of an election can be taken for granted. Indeed, Lee Kuan Yew once likened calling an election to a tossing of the political dice, a move no prime minister would make without first ensuring that everything possible had been done on the ground to raise the odds in his party's favour. In recent elections, several seats were won by margins of 5 percentage points or less, a close call each time. This is a clear sign of the integrity of the electoral process, as well as the importance of the votes you and I have.

Of course, elections alone do not make for a fully democratic society. Many other political practices, institutions, and attitudes are as important. But at a most fundamental level, the democratic voting rights which earlier generations of Singaporeans fought for are critical, and should not be undervalued. For so long as Singaporeans have the vote and are prepared to wield it effectively, politicians know that although they hold much power, it is not limitless in scope and in time, and ultimately, they must act within the bounds of what we, the people, find acceptable.

Even in Singapore, where the ruling party is dominant, many policies – from moves to raise the CPF withdrawal age, to changes to the bilingual education or censorship policies – are shaped with an eye on how it will go down with the voters (see page 69). Even in Singapore, the seemingly all-powerful PAP has had to pay heed to what has been called the 'political electoral cycle', timing unpopular measures such that they are implemented way before the polls and with sufficient time to show results, for voters to enjoy some of the gain from the dreaded pain they have been subjected to. Although politics in Singapore is less rambunctious than elsewhere, it is no less about balancing competing interests and concerns of various electoral, ethnic, income and interest groups. No government minister, I think, imagines that he can simply do as he chooses or deems fit, given his party's large parliamentary majority. The idea that there is no politics in Singapore is therefore one which seems to me to be eminently worth debunking.

The recent 'no turning the clock back' speech by Lee Hsien Loong is a case in point. Speaking to the Harvard Club of Singapore in January 2004, he made clear that the 'open consultative' style of government, which has become synonymous with Goh Chok Tong, would continue when he assumed the country's top job on August 12. Declaring that Singapore was now at a major transition point, he added, 'It is not just a changing of the guard. Our world has changed irrevocably, a younger generation born after independence is now in majority, and our strategies to grow our economy and root our people must change. Many Singaporeans ask: moving forward, will the society continue to open up? I have no doubt that our society must open up further. The growing participation and diversity over the last decades have been vital pluses for Singapore, enabling us to adapt to changing conditions and the needs and expectations of a new generation. They are key to providing Singaporeans an emotion anchor.'

It was a significant declaration, all the more so as it was made in one of his first major speeches after the announcement in August 2003 that he would be the next prime minister. Some Singaporeans will choose to be cynical. But I see no reason not to take Mr Lee at his word. Singapore's new prime minister took pains to show that he had been very much a part of the team behind the gradual liberalisation of discourse. Indeed, the liberalisation process reflects a trend that goes back to the 1980s and 1990s, when the PAP recognised that its style of engaging a more educated and politically demanding electorate had to change with the times.

This view was well encapsulated in the 1991 'pruning the banyan tree' speech by then Information and the Arts Minister George Yeo, in which he told a crowd of Singapore's English-educated intelligentsia that the government recognised the need to keep up with changes in society. It would open up Singapore further to the world, as many in the audience that night had urged, but at a pace that would enable it to hold the support of the more conservative majority as well. Then, as now, BG Yeo spoke of pruning the banyan tree of state, not quite felling it. Change, in other words, would come, in time, in an evolutionary, not revolutionary, fashion. More than a decade later, Mr Lee's Harvard speech said as much. Most Singaporeans, I believe, consider this approach to be sensible and sound.

Yet, herein lies the big paradox of Singapore politics: For all its electoral success, why is the People's Action Party, which has done so much to transform the country's fate and prospects, taking it from Third World to First in a generation, the subject of so much public ambivalence? It's a complex question, one that cannot be fully addressed in a brief essay. Part of the answer lies, of course, in the fact that government leaders have had, over the years, to take some difficult and unpopular decisions, such as raising the Goods and Services Tax or imposing fee hikes. But this explanation is both obvious and incomplete. Let me cite several deeper factors, which I think go some way to fleshing it out.

The first has to do with the fact that the PAP is a mass-based party which has long sought to represent the broad sweep of Singapore society. Its roots lie in the circle of English-educated intellectuals led by Lee Kuan Yew in the early years of the anti-colonial struggle, in the 1950s. Ever the master political strategist, he knew that to win and hold power, the PAP would have to secure the backing of the Chinese majority population in the country, with its deep-seated and relatively conservative views on how societies should be ordered and governed. Having learned his political lessons the hard way, in street battles with the communists and communalists, Mr Lee would never forget, nor allow his younger colleagues to do so. The PAP would not readily cede this ground to any challengers, even as it sought to modernise Singapore society. This tension between being the vanguards of modernisation and change, while upholding the country's traditional core, has been at the heart of the political balancing act that the PAP's leaders have had to perform through the years. Managing the painful process of change in a disparate society has long been one of the PAP's key political challenges, and remains so today.

One simple and neat way of highlighting the divergent forces that shape Singapore society, and the PAP's approach to holding sway over this diverse electorate, is to compare it with the segmented audiences that tune in to the main television stations that broadcast on the island. The Channel 5 crowd comprises the Housing Board heartlanders, many comfortable, if not fully competent, in English. Mostly concerned with bread and butter issues, they are also at home with developments around the world, increasingly outward-looking, tolerant and liberal. Channel 8 voters, the largest segment, refer to those in the Chinese-speaking HDB heartlands, who are generally more politically and socially conservative. Then there are the Arts Central voters, made up mostly of the English-educated elite, the cosmopolitans who went to top universities abroad, and travel frequently on business, or for their shopping sprees or annual holidays. This lot is most eager for change, to see society in Singapore embrace the values and practices of the globalising world.

Of course, this is no more than a rough and ready simplification. Indeed, over the years, there has been a growing overlap in 'viewership'. As more Singaporeans become familiar with the wider world, through education in English-language schools, frequent travel, contact with foreign visitors and workers in the city, and the growing use of the Internet, some views and attitudes of the various ethnic, economic, social and language groups in society on a range of issues have grown a little closer, even as some remain poles apart.

Even so, the Channel 5 and 8 distinction is a useful metaphor for reflecting how differently the various segments of society react to policies. Moves to liberalise censorship, for example, might appeal to the Arts Central crowd, but not the Channel 8 voters. The latter have grave doubts about the wisdom of going down this road. Not only are such moves seen as misguided, but some among this group also view them as a sign of weakness by the government, a needless pandering to the vocal minority. Arts Central voters might complain that the government is too 'paternalistic', endlessly intervening in people's lives, and Channel 5 voters might also want it to pull back a little. But Channel 8 voters are much less comfortable with recent suggestions that the government ought to 'do less' in some spheres, such as setting social norms or upholding values, or providing health care or education services and subsidies, fearing a situation with 'no government', or *boh cheng hu*, as the Hokkiens put it.

Faced with these conflicting pulls on them, to shore up their conservative electoral base, and perhaps because their basic instincts lie with them, some PAP politicians are wont to make statements that leave Channel 5 voters, not to mention the Arts Central ones, bewildered, perhaps even aghast. This results in reinforcing in some people's minds the party's image of being 'paternalistic', conservative, even heavy-handed.

This problem of having to satisfy disparate interest groups (economic, social, ethnic and language) is especially acute in a highly compact urban society – there is no clear distinction between the needs and interests of urban and rural voters, for instance – and presents a major challenge for anyone who would seek to mobilise voters across the political spectrum, especially in today's media age. The government – or some members of it – might wish to take a more relaxed attitude towards its critics, but it also thinks that some views must be countered to keep the majority of voters on its side.

On some issues or reforms, it might want to move more rapidly but it has to do so at a pace that the majority in society is comfortable with. Indeed, as the parliamentary gallery columnist for *The Straits Times* in the early 1990s, I recall the highlight of the annual budget debate being the address by then Information and the Arts Minister George Yeo. He would eloquently fend off vociferous calls from MPs belonging to the more conservative wing of the PAP demanding that the government do more to curb and check the proliferation of the Internet. They argued that the growing access to the Net would expose young Singaporeans to unhealthy liberal values and attitudes which would undermine the social fabric. Patiently, BG Yeo would repeat what became known as his 'open the windows, but keep out the flies' speech to try to persuade members of his own party that it was in Singapore's interest to be plugged into the wider world, even while doing all it could to uphold and promote Singapore's traditional values and practices.

These conflicting pulls in society, which the PAP has sought to manage, gives rise to the feeling among some that it is moving at a seemingly glacial pace when it comes to political and social reforms. But others are quite content, while some feel that changes are taking place too quickly for their liking. Unlike some parties elsewhere, which have a more clearly defined electoral base, the PAP's efforts to reflect the views of the broad sweep of the society results in many voters being less than fully satisfied.

Mixed channels and messages also arise when politicians seek to address the concerns of some groups in society, even if it means upsetting others. To prevent some ideas from taking root, confusing the public, or raising expectations among its mass base, some ministers think it is better to come out quickly to debunk them and demolish those who are advancing them. Hence, for example, the strong reaction to the suggestion by some academics in August 2003 that government policies favoured foreign talent ahead of Singaporeans. At a time of relatively high unemployment and considerable economic pain, PAP leaders must have sensed that if this view took hold, its standing with the people would have been badly damaged. It therefore chose to counter the arguments, even at the expense of alienating the liberal-minded minority, who saw the academics as doing no more than contributing to public discourse, which the government itself claimed it wanted to encourage. Similarly, when the Remaking Singapore Committee floated the idea that civil servants should work a five-day week, some ministers were quick to shoot it down, lest it take root, even at the risk of being seen to be dismissive of the committee's work. They argued that the idea of shutting down public services over the weekend was outmoded in today's 24/7 world, and did not want expectations to be raised among civil servants which might later need to be dashed.

This tension arising from mixed channel messaging is perhaps at its most acute at election time. The ruling party, in its determination not to lose any seats in Parliament, ups the ante and raises the stakes.

Changes are made to the electoral system, often announced just before the polls. Then, there are the ever-larger carrots and sticks, wielded for all to behold during the hustings. The PAP has shown a tendency to dramatise issues during the hustings along 'with me or against me' lines. Thus, political opponents are cast, not as people with different political views, but as 'opportunists', 'dangerous men', those who might not just disagree with the ruling party, but are out to undermine the entire political edifice.

No doubt some oppositionists have brought trouble on themselves, with the rash manner in which they too have chosen to up the ante, making libellous and scurrilous accusations during their campaigns. But this high tension politics, I think, leaves many Singaporeans – especially the better-educated, more liberal-minded groups – cold. Not a few are put off by the PAP's hardball tactics. Faced with little real choice, given the baleful state of the opposition – for which the PAP must surely take both credit and blame – the sense of alienation from the political process gets ratcheted up another notch.

Similarly, the PAP's long years of domination of Parliament and politics in general have given rise to the impression – rightly or wrongly – that it seeks to have the upper hand and win every argument. Over and again, government ministers have been known to warn, perhaps with too much seeming relish, that commentators risk getting a 'robust response' if they stray into a political minefield, wittingly or otherwise. That rubs many the wrong way.

Furthermore, the party's self-image is that of a tough-minded, businesslike, do-what-needs-to-be-done institution. Whereas the PAP's founding fathers recognised the need to win both hearts and minds in the 1950s and 1960s, the view among some Singaporeans today is that too often politicians seem to think that, ultimately, it is 'better to be feared than to be loved', to borrow a by now infamous line from Lee Kuan Yew, who was quoting Machiavelli.

How to change this? Well, that is for the PAP to ponder, if it wishes to continue to engage and be engaged by the voters.

Given the PAP's desire to continue to be the politically dominant centre party representing the broad majority of Singaporeans, its key challenge will remain that of accommodating various interests in society and managing the tensions between disparate groups. In doing so, it will be impossible to please everyone, all the time. That may be the PAP's – and Singapore's – political karma.

But perhaps there is still room for a bit of a remaking of Singapore politics, going beyond the old fear me or love me dichotomy. Goh Chok Tong showed the way at the Remaking Singapore event. He spoke his mind and stated his views, graciously welcoming the committee's ideas, while making clear that there were limits to how far and how rapidly some things could be changed. He signalled that good government was not always about simply taking the middle course between competing views. Even while allowing opposing sides to contend with one another, the government would ultimately have to reach a considered decision on the best way forward for the country. In the process, not all feedback or ideas thrown up could be accommodated or implemented. But that did not mean that the government was not listening or unwilling to hear alternative views and consider making changes where needed. Few, I think, would have disagreed with him that afternoon. He was comfortable and confident enough not to need to hide his sense of humour and the inherent humanness of his leadership. He showed that, sometimes, you can both lead and be liked, and perhaps all good leaders should strive to do a bit of both.

Indeed, in this regard, the success of relative newcomers to the political scene, like Health Minister Khaw Boon Wan and Second Minister for National Development Lim Swee Say, respected as much for their ability as their humility and their 'one of us' likeableness, is noteworthy. Voters, I believe, are likely to be willing to go along with more difficult political solutions if there is an underlying trust and a strong bond with their leaders.

At the end of the day, Singaporeans are pragmatic. They want good government. They recognise performance and respect those who are able to deliver on their political promises. The 'more free rice' and 'lower taxes, higher spending' brand of politics does not sway many when it comes to casting their ballots. But there is also a growing sense that people want to feel at home in their own country, comfortable with themselves, their society, and their leaders. No one wants to be at home, yet afraid.

Are democratic values and practices inborn and inherited, or can they be acquired and adapted? This issue was raised by Lee Kuan Yew in 1991. Taking up the question, I argued in a column published in May that year, that democratic values must underpin any attempt at liberal democracy. If they are not innate in a society, they can be acquired with the growth of a middle class. While doing so poses some problems, especially if some parts of the population are slow to embrace democratic values, adopting representative democracy is the best way for governments to forge a consensus with their peoples on the way forward.

'Liberal' democracy or not, popular support is essential

IN HIS speech to an *Asahi Shimbun* symposium in Tokyo, Senior Minister Lee Kuan Yew raised a fundamental question: Is democracy just a political system or a way of life? After all, you do not make a people democratic simply by introducing them to elections or political parties. These are no more than the trappings of liberal democracy, not its essential preconditions.

One precondition for democracy, however, might be political liberalism. This is not just a political philosophy, but also a political outlook, even a way of life. It entails the recognition that no view is immutably correct, that no one has a monopoly of wisdom, that no truth is universal or applicable for all time.

Such an outlook is often associated with a society that has reached a certain educational and economic level, one which has a sizeable middle class that is liberal in outlook and materially secure enough to accept democratic defeat at the ballot box. Or as the Senior Minister put it: 'For democracy to work, a people must acquire, if they have not inherited, cultural habits that make contending groups adjust differences or conflicts not by violence, but by give and take... People must have reached a certain high level of education and economic development ... and produced a sizeable middle class so that life is not such a fight for basic survival.' I agree with that.

It might be asked, what are these cultural habits that are necessary for democracy? Do we mean the culture of a particular race? Should we conclude that because the Russian people, of white Christian stock, have not acquired democratic impulses, democracy will therefore not come to Asian societies? I think not. For while race or ethnicity is, no doubt, an important factor which shapes a society's political practices, it is neither a necessary nor a sufficient factor for democracy. You do not have to be British, or even white, to be a democrat.

Culture here should be taken to refer instead to political cultures, or what Brigadier-General (NS) George Yeo calls 'cultural DNA' – the shared political and historical experiences of a people, which are deeply embedded in their collective memories through years of shared history. As Mr Lee rightly pointed out, one of the reasons why many Western commentators are pessimistic about the prospects for democracy in the Soviet Union is that Russia, having never experienced the European Renaissance in the 15th Century or the 17th Century Enlightenment, lacks the liberal civic society needed to underpin democracy. And if the Russians have not inherited democratic impulses, they are not now in a position to acquire them either. With the country rapidly plunging into economic catastrophe, minds there are more focused on when and from where the daily bread will come. The

Russians, at this time, are far from being a middle-class society in a liberal frame of mind.

This begs the question: can Asian peoples who have not had the political experiences of their Western counterparts expect democracy to come naturally? I think not. But while they may not inherit such democratic traits, they may, as Mr Lee argued, acquire them, adapting them along the way to suit their own unique circumstances. This seems to be the way Asia is going. Asian countries like the newly industrialising economies (NIEs), which have attained a high degree of economic success, are feeling the pressures for more representative government.

Yet liberal democratic impulses in these societies do not run deep. Many Asian societies, including Singapore, mirror, in varying degrees, the situation in China, where a liberal elite (for whom the democratic idea that man can govern himself is irresistible) is pitted against a large mass who would prefer to lead quiet lives and leave the hurly-burly of government to their 'betters'.

For this reason, the American credo that democracy is universally good is simplistic. It assumes that if 'primitive countries' would only emulate the American way of life and culture and adopt the trappings of democracy, they too will ascend to the democratic nirvana. Rather, the dilemma that Asian societies face now is this: how are they to make the transition to representative government demanded by the liberal elites when the majority of society has yet to acquire liberal instincts? For a headlong rush towards the liberal political paradise may well create tension that may undermine political stability, without which all further attempts at political liberalisation will be just so much political theory.

Yet, while this is a reminder of the need for caution, it is not sufficient reason for putting off the move towards a more open political system. As Mr Lee points out, especially in today's globally integrated world, governments must win popular backing if they are to galvanise the people into working together for the national good. Also, representative government is perhaps the best way for a society to forge a new consensus between the people and a new generation of leaders.

So the process of political development must continue if society here is to mature. Of course, this should not imply a blind aping of the West. We must build a political system in our own way and at our own pace, always conscious that this is a political experiment, which, unless handled carefully, may have explosive consequences.

(First published 13 May 1991)

The 1991 general election was a setback, not only for the PAP but also for those who favoured the trend towards a more liberal, tolerant political culture in Singapore. A disappointed Goh Chok Tong pledged that his party would close ranks and devise ways to make voters pay a price for choosing the opposition. But such hardball political tactics risked alienating more voters, I suggested in this piece in July 1992.

PAP should not read too much into by-election result

ALL MANNER of events, from the routine opening of the electoral register to news of the civil servants' three-month bonus, have been turned by pundits into indicators that by-elections are on the cards. This is hardly surprising. Not least after several political commentators said earlier this year that there could be as many as 10 to 12 opposition MPs here in the next 10 years.

The big question is how the PAP is likely to react to such a prospect. Of course, it is not preordained that the PAP will lose the by-elections. By carefully choosing its candidates, as well as the number and location of seats to be contested, it could well pull off a stunning victory. But that, as they say, is the 'rosy scenario'. Winning the by-elections will be an uphill battle, as it is for ruling parties everywhere.

What if the PAP should fail, and the opposition win more seats? Would this provoke a reaction from the PAP? Should it? These questions can be answered only if one knows the answer to another poser: How many opposition MPs is the PAP prepared to live with? No doubt, in a sense, the PAP will have to accept as many opposition MPs as the voters choose. But how will the ruling party react? Your guess is as good as mine.

Some clues can be gleaned from recent ministerial statements that suggest a desire to raise the stakes in the political battle. By tying priority for upgrading HDB flats with voting patterns, or transferring the HDB's emergency services to town councils, the party has served notice that it intends to make voters feel that there is a 'price' to be paid for voting for the opposition.

To be sure, some of these measures might have the beneficial effect of casting the opposition in a more managerial mould, forcing them to turn their minds to problems faced by any responsible party trying to run the country. This, I fear, is not how the moves are likely to be perceived on the ground. Instead, many will view them as still more measures to penalise people for not supporting the PAP. Some will be driven in pique into the arms of the opposition.

The PAP thus finds itself in a dilemma. To do nothing to stop the trend towards more voters backing the opposition could, it believes, lead ultimately to its undoing. Yet, to be seen to be striving too officiously to thwart them is also likely to bolster public sympathy for the opposition. What then is it to do? How should it respond to the political signals from the voters? Indeed, it might be asked, has it read those signals correctly?

We will never really know. Although there have been several speeches touching on the subject, the PAP's official analysis of its election performance remains a closely guarded secret. My own guess is that the party has not given enough credence to the so-called 'by-election effect', which some suggest was a major factor leading to its disappointing showing in last August's polls. Why is this important?

Well, because by-elections are hopelessly deceptive indicators of the public mood, as experience abroad should attest to. In most cases, voters know that the party in power is likely to form the government, even if it loses a seat or two. When voters sense that they can have their cake and eat it, they often choose to do so.

Now, if it is accepted that the last general election was, for most analytical purposes, a by-election, the folly of reacting unduly to the results will be apparent. Similarly, too much should not be made of the results of the upcoming by-elections. Instead of devising new schemes to get people to vote 'more wisely', the party would be better advised to accept that while most Singaporeans support it, many might also want more opposition MPs in the House.

The two positions are not mutually exclusive. To be sure, it is not the job of the PAP to help the opposition get elected. Nor is anyone expecting the PAP to declare openly that it is willing to see more opposition MPs in the House. In any case, the idea is not as outlandish as it may seem. After all, did not former Cabinet Minister S. Rajaratnam declare in 1988 that having six intelligent opposition MPs in the House would give the legislature a boost?

The obvious question that follows is this: Just how many opposition MPs would be 'tolerable'? Ten, 20, 30, even 40? There is no arbitrary line that can be drawn. Indeed, the PAP's worst fear must be that having a few more opposition MPs might create an unstoppable momentum that carries another party into power. Few, I think, believe that this is likely to happen soon, given the present crop of opposition candidates. But, by closing its ranks and becoming more politically belligerent, the PAP risks driving the very people who could pose the greatest danger to its electoral support into opposition ranks. That, ironically, would be a case of the PAP winning the electoral skirmish, but losing the political battle.

(First published 5 July 1992)

Elections in Singapore have generally been considered to be free and fair. This is a precious asset, which should be guarded jealously. Hence moves to amend electoral rules to create ever bigger GRC teams or changes to the electoral boundaries, which come just before the polls are called, leave an unfortunate impression among many that the PAP has resorted to changing the rules to win at the polls. This is especially unfortunate, I argued in October 1996, since it hardly needs to.

GRC changes risk being seen as tied to coming polls

AND THEN there were six.

A much speculated-about Bill introduced in Parliament yesterday by Prime Minister Goh Chok Tong will increase the number of MPs elected as a team in a Group Representation Constituency from the present four to six, if passed into law. It also sets a minimum of eight single-seat wards, lower than the present provisions, which state that no more than three-quarters of the total number of seats in the House can be won through GRCs. This works out to there having to be at least 20 single-seat wards in the present House of 81 MPs.

It took no more than five minutes for Mr Goh to go through the formal parliamentary procedures to introduce the Bill. This passed quickly and quietly enough. But at the back of my mind, I can almost hear the howls of protest from the opposition and some non-partisan Singaporeans, which will surely follow. The crux of the issue is this: Are the amendments aimed at modifying the electoral system to achieve the goals spelt out by the government, or are they an electoral sleight of hand, designed to boost the ruling party's chances at the coming general elections?

For his part, Mr Goh has, in recent statements outside the House, suggested that the amendments are tied to his proposal to form Community Development Councils and introduce mayors to promote community bonding, an idea he introduced in his National Day Rally speech in August. This appears to be an extension of the original rationale for GRCs mooted in 1987 by then backbencher Lim Boon Heng, who argued that having teams of three MPs elected together would give them the mandate to run a town council, which could then take decisions to improve residents' lives.

Later, it was added that GRCs would also ensure minority representation in the House, as one of the MPs on the slate was required to come from an ethnic minority group. In 1990, the Constitution was amended to raise the number of MPs on a GRC slate to four, while the proportion of MPs that could be elected through GRCs was raised from half to three-quarters. The reason given then was to enable GRCs to be expanded by an additional MP to cope with increases in their population size.

Taken at face value, these objectives seem sensible enough. After all, town councils have introduced many changes and made life better for residents. GRCs have also ensured ethnic representation in the House. As wards grow in size, more MPs might be needed, as might be changes in boundaries to ensure a good fit between town councils – or CDCs – and GRCs.

Yet, whether these grounds are sufficient to extend GRCs to having six MPs to a slate, while also limiting the number of single-seat wards to just eight is, at best, moot. What next? some will wonder. If MPs can be elected six at a go, why not 8, 10, or even more? And could the day when all MPs are elected as GRC teams be very far off?

Those who support GRCs on principle might well counter: Whyever not? Perhaps because underlying many of these questions is the nagging concern, shared by not a few, that the measures are designed to make it tougher for the opposition to win at the polls, by requiring them to form ever-bigger teams, which have to include a designated minority candidate. Perhaps also because the reduction in the number of single-seat wards will work against the opposition, for all of the seats won by opposition parties since 1988 have been single-seat wards.

Yet, GRCs might prove to be double-edged swords for the PAP. Indeed, in a few cases, opposition parties did come stunningly close to winning, such as in Eunos GRC in 1988, when a Workers' Party team polled 49.1 per cent of the valid votes, and again in that ward in 1991, when it won 47.6 per cent. Even against a relatively weaker team from the National Solidarity Party, the PAP team in Tampines GRC in 1991 won with just 59.5 per cent of the valid votes. Clearly, if opposition parties were able to band together to put up a few strong slates, it might pull off an upset and take six seats in a swoop, while unseating a sitting minister to boot.

One would have thought that this would be enough of a prize to prod them into putting aside petty personal and partisan rivalries, to form an alliance of sorts against the PAP. But given the fractious nature of the opposition parties here, which in recent months have been wont to split into more rival factions, this does seem rather unlikely.

That is its loss, which no doubt the PAP will revel in.

The most troubling aspect of the Bill, therefore, lies in the cynicism that could set in if Mr Goh and his team do not succeed in convincing Singaporeans that the amendments were not being moved with a prime ministerial eye on the impending polls. Indeed, it would be a great pity if, despite his government being well ahead in the race, and given its enviable track record over the last five years, the view was to take root that the PAP had resorted to changing the rules to win the game.

(First published 2 October 1996)

The 2001 general election marked a major victory for the PAP. Voters turned to the familiar in uncertain times. But many were also watching to see if the massive majority that the party won would lead it to rule with a light touch, showing confidence and openness to alternative views, I contended in this column after the elections in November 2001. Or would it use its untrammelled power in a less benign fashion?

Will a dominant PAP also be domineering?

WHAT is one to make of the November 3 polls result, in which three out of every four voters cast their lot with the ruling People's Action Party? In doing so, they handed the party a massive 10-percentage point swing, almost reversing the historic 12-percentage point turn against it in 1984.

One key factor stands out in explaining the PAP's resounding victory: timing. Given the deep sense of anxiety among voters over jobs and the economy, Prime Minister Goh Chok Tong chose his moment well to put to them one overriding question: Who can lead the country out of this crisis? Singaporeans, being pragmatic, backed a tried-and-tested team. Timing also explains how the opposition found itself wrong-footed, with little opportunity to marshal their limited and disparate forces to mount any kind of meaningful challenge. The result – 65.5 per cent of the seats uncontested, leaving more than half of all voters without an opportunity to exercise their democratic rights, an outcome that even PAP leaders lamented.

Without taking away anything from the strong endorsement that PM Goh and his team won, some fundamental questions arise about

Singapore's fledgling democracy, the kind of opposition that people here want (if at all), and what this might mean for the ruling party.

CONSIDER THE CASE of Singapore Democratic Alliance candidate Sin Kek Tong. Five years ago, I interviewed him at a press conference held at an HDB void deck, in the run-up to the 1997 elections. What plans, I asked, do you have for Braddell Heights, the ward he hoped to contest. 'I have no plans,' he replied cheerfully, insisting that he was only an opposition candidate. Out of desperation, my colleagues and I threw him a lifeline. What about upgrading, covered walkways, better transport? 'Yes, yes, I will do that,' he replied. 'Any more ideas?'

Not surprisingly, Mr Sin polled just 26.8 per cent of the valid votes in Ayer Rajah, which he moved to after Braddell Heights was absorbed into Marine Parade GRC. He had no plans for Ayer Rajah either. I was amused to see Mr Sin back again in 2001, declaring with breathtaking audacity that, if elected in Jalan Besar GRC, he would implement the plans that had already been drawn up by his PAP opponents!

Guess how much Mr Sin and his team polled this time: 25.5 per cent. I have no idea whether he plans to withdraw from politics, as he threatens to do from time to time, or if he will contest the 2007 elections. If he does, he should come more prepared to face the voters, who deserve better than his 'I am just the opposition' line. Even assuming that he aims only to be a voice of the people, they will want to know where he stands on key issues, and why.

Nor, I think, do voters want the fire and brimstone approach of the Singapore Democratic Party's Chee Soon Juan, casting aspersions and allegations on all he beholds. It would not be too much of an exaggeration to say that Dr Chee single-handedly dashed his SDP team's chances – and perhaps dampened those of other opposition candidates as well – with one foolish outburst against PM Goh one fateful Sunday morning. It used to be conventional wisdom among political watchers here that 25 to 30 per cent of the electorate would back an opposition candidate, even if it was Ah Meng the orangutan who stood against the PAP, so deep was the desire for a check on the ruling party. November 3 changed all that. Dr Chee and his SDP teams in Jurong and Hong Kah GRC polled just about 20 per cent of the vote, raising questions about his claim to speak on behalf of Singaporeans. In contrast, the more moderate stance taken by the SDA saw it garnering 25 per cent or more in Jalan Besar and Tampines GRCs, a tad above the national average.

To my mind, opposition candidates should pass the 'Walter Woon test' – they should have minds of their own, with clear and credible ideas, but yet be moderate, humble and sincere in their desire to further the public interest. SDA chief Chiam See Tong and Workers' Party head Low Thia Khiang came closest to meeting this mark. Their victories are all the more significant when set against the nationwide 10-percentage point swing to the PAP, and the fact that the PAP big guns had joined the fray against them. In contrast, candidates like those from the Democratic Progressive Party, the 'slipper men' of Singapore politics, got the thrashing they deserved. Singapore's discerning and demanding electorate wants more than candidates who saunter into nomination centres, put in their papers, and then are never heard of again.

This is why I disagree with the cries that rang out over the $13,000 deposit required for each candidate. After all, holding an election is a serious and costly business. Resources have to be mobilised to organise the voting, counting and tallying of ballots, not to mention the time and effort of those who have to cast their votes. Having a deposit is a means of ensuring that while elections are open to all, candidates who are not serious are sufficiently deterred. By the time the next election comes round, the deposits may well rise with inflation to, say, $15,000 – maybe more. This means potential candidates will have four to five years to raise that amount, or about $3,000 or so a year; not a phenomenal sum. They should be able to raise this if indeed they have support on the ground.

More serious, however, are the opposition charges over the changes to the shape and size of the electoral boundaries, and the fact that these were unveiled just days before the elections. PM Goh has said that this cuts both ways, since PAP MPs and activists also had to regroup in a hurry after the new boundaries were made known. Still, there can be little doubt that opposition parties have a harder time doing so, especially if the ground they had been canvassing is wiped away from beneath them. Perhaps Mr Chiam or Mr Low, or even one of the Nominated MPs, should take up the issue in Parliament and call for a review of the Parliamentary Elections Act.

To my mind, it would be fairer if the act required boundary changes to be gazetted at least a month before Nomination Day, to give all candidates sufficient time to decide on their strategy and to work the ground. The PAP, no doubt, will be loath to give up this tactical advantage. But it would be wise to do so, to be seen to be fair in giving ample opportunity to its rivals to put up a proper challenge, rather than merely lamenting the lack of one after the event. Otherwise cynicism about the political process might well set in.

TO HAVE GARNERED 75 per cent of the vote and a near clean sweep in the 2001 elections was no mean feat in this day and age, even for the PAP. It raises the question of just how the PAP is going to repeat this victory in 2007, when a new man might be leading the party into the polls. Will failure to do so be seen as a setback? A repudiation of the new team? That would be unfortunate, not least for the blow it will deal to the process of political transition here. Worse, there is the danger that if the PAP gets caught in the numbers game and becomes hell-bent on repeating the feat, it may well end up upping the ante at election time to try to do so. That would be foolhardy. In the absence of a national crisis, no party should regard a clean sweep at the polls as a matter of course, especially in a highly educated and urbanised electorate. Broad as the PAP church might be, there must be room in a democracy for other voices, other views.

Indeed, just how the PAP deals with its huge majority in the new Parliament will also be watched closely by Singaporeans, who might wonder if a dominant PAP will mean a domineering one. After losing four seats in 1991, a despondent Mr Goh declared that the party would now have to 'close ranks'. Will this resounding victory mean that the party will be able to take a more relaxed view towards dissenting voices, both inside and outside the House?

The proposal for a People's Action Forum appears to be a step in this direction. But it does not go far enough. Limiting robust debate to just 20 MPs, with a partial lifting of the whip, seems scarcely different from the past practice of having Government Parliamentary Committees. To make a real difference, it would be better for the PAP to allow all its MPs to speak and vote their minds, with the whip being deployed only for crucial votes, as is the case with parties elsewhere. (Few parties have a whip applied across the board; most would never be able to pull it off anyway.) Doing so would give a much needed boost to parliamentary debates, without threatening the PAP all that much. It has a big enough majority to carry its agenda through, and most of its MPs would still vote with the government anyway. What it would do is send a clear signal to MPs and voters alike that the government is committed when it says that it wants to remake the country and that all policies are up for review.

After all, despite the fact that most voters plumped for the PAP to pull the country out of recession, many will still want a say in how the society is to be reshaped in the longer term. Voters will thus be watching to see if the PAP is able not only to deliver on its electoral promises, but also if it will do so in a spirit of openness to ideas, tolerance of diversity and general good grace.

(First published 10 November 2001)

Bathtub syndrome

Look into many Singaporean homes, including HDB flats, and what do you find? Bathtubs! Yet most Singaporeans, myself included, hardly ever choose to soak in a tub. A bathtub, I gather, costs between a few hundreds to thousands of dollars. Multiply that by the hundreds of thousands of households here, and you will realise just how much of a waste of space and resources these little-used luxuries are.

How on earth did Singaporeans find themselves sucked in by the 'bathtub syndrome'? Someone, somewhere, must have started this trend, which caught on, so much so that bathtubs are now added to new homes almost as a matter of course. Walk into new condominium show flats these days and what will you find? Not just bathtubs, but also two sinks in the bathrooms – 'to prevent disputes between husband and wife', one brochure declared – and even bidets and jacuzzis. Nothing wrong with that. But ask yourself: Who wants them? How much? And who's paying?

(From 'Internet in cabs: Nice to have, but who pays?'
7 July 2001, see page 61)

Chapter 2
What price politics?

THE NEW HDB Hub sits on the site of the old Toa Payoh bus interchange. Having grown up in that Housing Board estate, where I lived for more than a decade, I remember it well. My daily trip to school would begin and end at the hot, dusty, smoky interchange, which was not a place to linger in longer than you needed to. The new hub comes complete with air-conditioned bus bays, where commuters wait in cool comfort for their bus to arrive. The centre is linked to the MRT station and to an array of shops, supermarkets and cinemas. Competition has been brewing among hip coffee joints and fancy bakeries, which charge as much as $3 or more for a cup of coffee, or more than a dollar for a bun or confection with unusual names, up from 20 to 30 cents for these treats in the old days. Funny thing is, despite the high prices, people are slurping up lattes and snapping up 'applewerms' (yes, an apple-flavoured bun shaped like a worm).

This used to be called the HDB heartland, but these days such suburban town centres bear a growing resemblance to the downtown city malls just a 10 minute MRT ride away. My favourite among these is Orchard Cineleisure. Despite being a few years old, this place remains hip and happening, with its all-night movie screenings, its ever-changing menu of eateries, including the trendy sidewalk café where diners are cooled by blowers that bathe them in a gentle spray to keep the tropical heat at bay. The place reminds me of the past as much as the future. The bright young people who frequent it and its new state-of-the-art movie halls offer a glimpse of things to come. But today's Orchard Cineleisure, with its funny name, has a special resonance for me, as I recall clearly the old Orchard cinema that used to stand on its very site. Then, too, it was a happening hangout, where couples and the young at heart went for a night out. A movie ticket would have set you back $1, or $1.50. Today, it costs about $7. Then again, movies back then were months-old blockbusters such as the *Towering Inferno* or *Jaws*, unlike today when some films are screened the day that they premier in Hollywood or London. Then, we sat on hard wooden or leather seats, unlike the plush theatres of today, with their soft carpeting, fancy lighting and THX sound systems.

This story of rising costs and spiralling expectations has been a leitmotif of Singapore politics in recent years. Singaporeans lament how costly the country has become and how stressful it is to keep up with the never-ending cycle of upgrading. From computers to cars, handphones to hairdos, there is always a new model that you have to have. Costs rise, with all manner of things becoming less affordable along the way.

Similarly, public services have kept pace with this endless cycle of upgrading. Housing Board blocks now have soft lighting and talking lifts – though why anyone needs a lift to talk to him has always been a mystery to me. Indeed, the swish new HDB headquarters in Toa Payoh, where people go to book subsidised public housing, with its plasma display screens and plush waiting areas, is far fancier than the corporate offices of some private property developers. Public hospitals offer much the same creature comforts as private ones, which aim to be 'hotels for the sick'. Public transport operators aim to outdo each other with new services, such as satellite systems to track their taxis or Internet access for passengers riding in their taxis. The result: rising costs, and fees and charges that go up and up.

To be fair, the biggest cost push comes from rising wages and salary expectations, but the 'frills' that people demand and later come to expect as 'standard' fare also jack up costs. For example, it never fails to amuse me to see the pretty store displays of the latest bed linen on sale, complete with duvet and pillow shams. Why, you might wonder, do people need duvets in tropical Singapore? Well, simply because many have grown used to sleeping in air-conditioned comfort, which leads to them needing a duvet. I confess the bedroom sets look ever so smart and alluring in today's modern bedrooms, though the cost might give you a restless night.

Little wonder then that the cost of living issue is almost always one of the most significant issues whenever Singaporeans go to the polls. Just about every election is about bread-and-butter issues, although in reality most Singaporeans have long moved on to kaya and jam, if not muffins and lattes. When times were good, expectations ratcheted up and more and more people got used to having the trappings of the good life. When times turned bad, as in recent years, people found it difficult to part with them. It is the source of much contention. Every Singaporean wants somebody, somewhere to do something about it. But not with any compromises to the high standards of service we are accustomed to.

Therein lies the rub. Singaporeans' expectations have risen to First World levels, far outstripping our willingness to pay for the newfound services. In the present difficult times, some Singaporeans have lost their ability to pay. They are the most deserving of help, but are not always the ones who get the most help, being less vocal about their plight than the more articulate middle classes. How to wean Singaporeans off these high cost, but lowly priced goods and services will be a recurring theme of politics in the years ahead, as some segments of the population are forced to make painful adjustments, downgrading to a more sustainable standard of living.

Even in Singapore, with a dominant party in power, the government has had to resort to raising fees slowly but surely in good years, well ahead of any sign of an election. It has also come up with clever schemes to get Singaporeans to be more willing to pay for some of their luxuries. For example, since almost every young couple now aspires to a five-room HDB flat – unlike their parents who were grateful to move from humble villages to three-room flats with running water and modern sanitation – the size of five-room flats has gradually been reduced in recent years, so that more can enjoy these 'bigger' flats in land-scarce Singapore. And as public housing has lost its cachet with a more affluent younger generation, more couples are being enticed to buy executive or low-end private housing. These do not come with the huge subsidies that are given for Housing Board flats, and so are less of a strain on the national coffers. Similarly, more young couples, taking advantage of the availability of Medisave funds, are choosing to have their babies delivered in cosier private hospitals, instead of turning to heavily subsidised public ones.

These trends will continue as a growing proportion of Singaporeans become tertiary-educated and so aspire to the 'good life' to which they think their university degree entitles them. But whereas university graduates were a privileged few in the past, as the number of graduates rises, competition for the plumb jobs, choice locations for homes and luxury cars will inevitably grow. A university degree, in itself, will no longer be a sure ticket to the 'good life'. Besides, as expectations rise and pressures mount on the system to deliver, people are increasingly going to have to be told that they must bear a greater share of the costs of the high quality public services they want, while also setting aside something for their future.

For nearly two decades, the government has been grappling with this last headache: how to get more Singaporeans to make adequate provision for their retirement. Most people assume that their needs will be provided for by their Central Provident Fund savings. But as people live longer, and as medical costs rise, many are just not going to have enough CPF savings to maintain their standard of living once they retire. Valiant efforts have been made to tackle this looming problem, starting with the much criticised Howe Yoon Chong Committee report in the mid-1980s, which hinted at plans to raise the CPF withdrawal age. But a public uproar caused the idea to be dropped, with politicians finding other 'softly, softly' ways to do the needful, which many commentators lamented did not go far enough. It was only in 2003, in the wake of the strong public backing for the government during the Sars crisis, that a window of opportunity opened, to make a major overhaul of the CPF system politically feasible.

The new mantra is that of personal choice, which comes with responsibility. The government, responding to public calls to be less of a nanny state, seems only too keen to cut some of the apron strings. So whether it is public housing, health care or education, public provision would be focused on the most needy, with more and more Singaporeans being asked to pay more of their own way for the higher quality services they desire or have grown accustomed to. The question is: are Singaporeans ready to say goodbye to reliable, familiar old nanny?

Public services in Singapore are constantly upgrading to higher standards and costs. This has raised questions about whether the new services provided are wasteful and desired by the public. Services might be 'affordable', and yet more than what the public are willing to pay.

Internet in cabs:
Nice to have, but who pays?

IT MUST have seemed like a brilliant idea. After all, many Singaporeans spend hours every day surfing the Net and checking their e-mail. Since people have a bit of time to kill while travelling in a cab, why not let them roam far and wide virtually? Marvellous! So, enter CityCab's plan to conduct a trial run for high-speed Internet access for passengers in 500 of its 5,000 taxis by the end of the year. The cost – a cool $15 million.

Public reaction came at Internet speed. Trash it, was the common view. Use the money instead to improve service, making taxis available when people need them and drivers more willing to lend passengers a helping hand.

Said Joseph Mok, 48, an accountant: 'Surfing the Net usually takes a longer time than a cab ride. It is unnecessary technology.' NSman Chan Yien Fong, 23, agreed: 'We don't need fanciful gadgets. We just want taxi companies to fulfil their role as a transport provider – a role they've not performed well.' Even cabby Neo Kim Khuw, 45, argued: 'Although it's a good idea, the operator should maybe channel the money to more pressing matters, such as reducing taxi rentals and easing the peak hour taxi shortage.'

These reactions are hardly surprising, and they have been aired before. When public hospitals began in the late 1980s to introduce fancy carpets and fittings to match the claims of private hospitals of being 'hotels for the sick', the public sniffed at the development and baulked at having to cough up the higher charges. Similarly, in the 1990s, some town councils learnt the hard way that their moves to introduce elaborate fountains, landscaping and soft lighting came with higher maintenance costs and so, ultimately, higher charges for residents.

In each of these cases, the public service providers were caught up by a nifty idea and neglected to ask three golden questions: Who wants it? How much? And who's paying? These caveats are essential, for any public service once provided has a way of rapidly entrenching itself, giving rise to a ratcheting up of expectations and demands from the public.

I like to call this the 'bathtub syndrome'. What do I mean? Well, look into many Singaporean homes, including HDB flats, and what do you find? Bathtubs! Yet most Singaporeans, myself included, hardly ever choose to soak in a tub. A bathtub, I gather, costs between a few hundreds to thousands of dollars. Multiply that by the hundreds of thousands of households here, and you will realise just how much of a waste of space and resources these little-used luxuries are. Now, I often wonder, how on earth did Singaporeans find themselves sucked in by the 'bathtub syndrome'? Someone, somewhere, must have started this trend, which caught on, so much so that bathtubs are now added to new homes almost as a matter of course. Walk into new condominium show flats these days and what will you find? Not just bathtubs, but also two sinks in the bathrooms – 'to prevent disputes between husband and wife', one brochure declared – and even bidets and jacuzzis. Nothing wrong with that. But ask yourself: Who wants them? How much? And who's paying?

Indeed, even the two new HDB Punggol 21 show flats at Block 105C, Edgefield Plains reportedly feature an impressive array of facilities, including Internet-enabled appliances, surveillance cameras, motion detectors which switch on lights and air-conditioning, and a single master remote control. These extras, however, do not come free. The equipment and wiring needed could cost about $6,000 a flat. Thankfully, the HDB is conducting a survey to see if there is indeed demand for such optional extras. Yet, I cannot help but wonder how long it is before these 'extras' become necessities, which the public is said to demand, thereby adding to the inexorable rise in the cost of public housing, which everybody, no doubt, will lament.

The public sector should aim to deliver services that are 'cheap and good' when it comes to satisfying the basic needs of citizens for health, housing and transport. This would minimise the drain on taxpayers' resources and, thereby, keep taxes down. Only these basic services should be subsidised, leaving individuals free to choose to pay for the frills if they want them.

One example of this principle was recently featured in the July issue of *Home and Decor* magazine, which ran a story of a young professional couple who spent $70,000 renovating their five-room HDB flat, knocking down walls and creating 'options for socialising with friends – corners to chat, expandable space for parties and a cosy area for karaoke and movies'. And of course, room enough for Lassie, their collie, to have a good romp. The expenditure seemed frivolous. But then again, what a young couple chooses to spend their hard-earned money on is really up to them. So long as they don't turn around and complain about the rising cost of housing here, demand more subsidies – paid for with your tax dollar and mine – to keep public housing 'affordable'.

The policy conundrum that arises here is this: Even as people gripe about the cost of public housing, how is it that many who buy highly subsidised HDB flats spend tens, if not hundreds, of thousands on renovations? Perhaps it is because the HDB flats are in great need of renovation. But is it because buyers have money to spare thanks to the heavy subsidies they enjoy? If they did not, forking out more on renovations would scarcely be possible.

The choice of whether to spend on expensive karaoke party rooms or multiple Internet points should really be up to those who own these flats. Such extras should not be part of the basic service that public agencies are expected to provide or subsidise. The challenge for public service providers should thus be to deliver services that are both 'good' and 'affordable', with an eye firmly on getting the basics right. Of course the criteria will change over time, in line with the rise in standards of living. When they do, 'sense of vision' should be balanced with the very real need to have a 'sense of reality', as the Shell rating qualities go. Having one or the other alone will not do. By all means, dare to dream. But not all dreams can or need to be turned into reality. Before rushing to do so, public service providers would do well to pause, sit in their bathtubs, and repeat the million-dollar mantra: Who wants it? How much? Who's paying?

(First published 7 July 2001)

For all its 'no free lunch' free-market rhetoric, the PAP government is remarkably socialist, handing out large subsidies for housing, health care and education. Some subsidies are also targeted to win political support, raising the question of what and who subsidies should really be for, and where to draw that crucial line.

Who should gain from subsidies?

A RECENT survey of Singaporean attitudes to welfare policies revealed some disturbing differences among the population here. Consider these findings:

❖ Whereas 91 per cent of those who own one- to three-room Housing Board flats, and 85 per cent of four- and five-roomers backed the government's proposal to give $30,000 grants to couples who wish to buy a resale flat in the same estate as their parents, only 64 per cent of private property owners welcomed it.

❖ More than nine in 10 of those polled in all housing types backed the government's programme to upgrade older estates. But its interim upgrading programme, which aims to spruce up newer flats aged between 10 and 17 years, received less universal support. About 78 per cent of those in one- to three-room HDB flats and 74 per cent of four- and five-roomers welcomed the scheme. But only 55 per cent of private property owners did so, the survey by Singapore Press Holding's Research and Information department found. Similarly, some other asset-enhancement schemes introduced recently by the government, such as the sale of HDB shops and the topping up of Central Provident Fund accounts, also received far less support among better-off Singaporeans, assuming a close link between income levels and housing type.

These figures, I think, suggest a creeping subsidy fatigue among better-off Singaporeans. This is hardly surprising. Most Singaporeans appear not to begrudge those staying in older HDB estates an enhanced living environment. But they might be forgiven for baulking at having to fork out tax dollars for residents in newer HDB estates to enjoy faster lifts and covered walkways, under the $120 million a year interim upgrading programme. Especially when private property owners have to foot the bill for any repairs to their condominiums or houses.

Even more perplexing, however, is the finding that middle-class Singaporeans were most likely to think that the government was not giving out enough subsidies. Just over half, or 54 per cent, of those in four- and five-room HDB flats thought the present level of government subsidies was adequate, compared with 71 per cent of those in private property. Even one- to three-room HDB flat owners were more satisfied than the four-and five-roomers, with 65 per cent of them saying the present subsidies were sufficient.

The answer to why the middle classes should feel less happy about the levels of subsidies might lie in the figures cited recently by Prime Minister Goh Chok Tong. He pointed out that low and lower-middle income households, which have monthly incomes of $700 and $2,100 respectively, and together make up 70 per cent of all households here, gain about $20,000 more in benefits a year than the taxes they paid. In contrast, the 20 per cent of upper-middle-income households, with incomes of $4,500 a month, enjoy a net gain of $4,000 a year. Upper-income households earning $9,700 a month paid about $14,000 a year more in taxes than the benefits they received from the government, he noted.

Mr Goh also wondered why some Singaporeans were so unhappy despite the healthy economic growth here in recent years. His answer: Singaporeans' expectations had risen faster than the rate at which their incomes grew each year, thereby leaving some without the means to satisfy their new desires. The R and I survey findings indicate that this phenomenon of rising incomes lagging behind mounting expectations is especially true of the middle classes. Those in this group enjoy fewer subsidies, but harbour greater hopes of moving up in the world. So when prices of the things they desire – such as private property or cars – rise rapidly, they are more likely than their less well-off counterparts to feel that the good life is slipping beyond their grasp.

The crucial question: Should the government increase subsidies to placate them and ease the so-called 'middle-class squeeze'? Will it not face political pressure to do so? Indeed, whereas 50 per cent of those in private property saw subsidies as a means to win more votes for the government, 66 per cent of four- and five-room flat owners believed this to be so. One wonders if the converse is not also true. That is, that the middle classes may be prepared to use their votes as a means of extracting more benefits from the government, regardless of the consequences of doing so for the society as a whole.

That would be a pity indeed. For one man's subsidy is another's tax burden. The survey findings cited above indicate that there is clearly a limit to how much the government can tax the better-off to help others in society, without their wondering about the wisdom, and justice, of paying still more taxes.

Besides, the experience of the welfare states in the West shows that benefits that are paid universally, instead of being targeted at the most needy, have an uncanny way of ending up benefiting the middle classes, since the latter knows best how to make the most of the system. The result: welfare costs rise, but the least well-off in society often do not get the help they need. And, as the middle classes make up what American economist John Kenneth Galbraith calls the 'contented majority', attempts to scale back such benefits are all but impossible politically.

So, certainly, the government here will have to take steps to improve the public transport system, keep medical costs down, and provide good education at affordable rates, to meet the needs of the middle classes.

But the unavoidable fact is that as more Singaporeans attain tertiary education – one in six of each year's Primary 1 cohort will do so – many more will join the ranks of the middle classes and aspire to their trappings. Not all, however, can, or will, be satisfied. When political pressure mounts from this group for more government assistance, Singaporeans will do well to be clear about the primary aim of state welfare and subsidies. That is, to help the least well-off, not buy off the middle classes.

(First published 25 September 1994)

For many years, the government has been attempting to fix the Central Provident Fund system to ensure that most Singaporeans have enough savings for their retirement. But overwhelming public opposition to any change to the system has caused it to back down from radical reform. In August 2003, however, in the face of strong public support for the decisive way in which it tackled the Sars crisis, the government decided to embark on the most sweeping changes to the CPF in decades.

Many unprepared for retirement, even with CPF changes

WARNING: You need to sit down before reading on. Three stark and startling trends loom ahead of you. You need to deal with them.

Trend one: There will be 796,000 Singaporeans aged 65 and above by the year 2030, more than three times the number in 1999. By 2030, there will be only three working adults to provide for each retiree, down from 10 workers for every retiree in 2000. More of these elderly people will live longer; more will be single and have to provide for themselves.

Trend two: Although many more Singaporeans are going on to tertiary education these days, a staggering seven in 10 of those aged 65 to 74, or just over 350,000 people, will still have no more than lower secondary education in 2030. They will face difficulties doing the increasingly skilled jobs of the future in the run-up to their retirement.

Trend three: Figures from the Central Provident Fund Board in 2000 show that over 600,000 CPF members – about half the total number – have less than $80,000 in their CPF accounts, the minimum sum that they will be required to keep in their accounts by July next year.

Taken together, these three trends make for an ageing population that will be increasingly ill-prepared to provide for their retirement in the decades to come.

This nightmare scenario has plagued government leaders for many years, with several attempts being made to grapple with it since the 1980s. The first was the ill-fated Howe Yoon Chong Committee on the problems of the aged in 1984. Its wide-ranging report became known for just one thing: the proposal to raise the withdrawal age for CPF contributions from 55 to 60 or 65, which sparked a hue and cry. Lamenting this, then Second Deputy Prime Minister S. Rajaratnam said, 'It would be easier for the present government to ignore this problem and keep you living in a fool's paradise. But it would be cowardly of the government to do this because the price of our cowardice will have to be paid for by Singaporeans now under 40 and the succeeding generations waiting in the wings to be born.'

The public uproar, however, caused the idea to be dropped. What followed was a host of other review groups, which sought to learn from the Howe Committee's experience and find ways to tackle the problem without stirring up a major rumpus. In 1986, the CPF minimum sum scheme was unveiled. This was a 'softly, softly' way around the ageing problem. Instead of stopping CPF members from withdrawing their funds at 55, it allowed them to do so, provided they set aside a minimum sum – part cash, part property – which would rise gradually over the years to $80,000 by 2003. It was one of those art-of-the-possible compromises, based on what the public would wear, so to speak.

Yet, most experts recognise that even the $80,000 minimum sum would not be adequate, as it would mean retirees having just a few hundred dollars to get by each month. This would imply a sharp fall in their post-retirement living standards, since most economists recommend a retirement income of 70 per cent of a person's last-drawn salary, way above what the minimum sum would provide.

The problem thus remained, as Singaporeans continued to plough ever more of their CPF savings into properties, which panel after panel of experts had sounded warnings about from as early as the mid-1980s. In 1996, the Cost Review Committee, of which I was a member, pointed in its report to trends which

> 'raise serious questions for Singaporeans to ponder: Just what was the role of the government in providing public housing? Was the Housing Board in danger of being moved, by rising public expectations, beyond its originally intended role?
>
> 'Most significantly, were Singaporeans collectively over-investing in housing, at the expense of other more productive sectors? Indeed, what would happen should the property boom take a turn for the worse? Worse, who would buy the tens of thousands of flats that Singapore was now building annually when the population aged and demand for housing fell in the years to come?'

The man at the helm of the CRC was Lim Boon Heng, Minister of State Without Portfolio – the same man who caused a stir recently when he wondered aloud if Singaporeans were not over-investing in housing, incurring huge interest payments in the process, at the expense of saving for their retirement years.

Now, the Economic Review Committee sub-committee led by Senior Minister of State Tharman Shanmugaratnam has taken another stab at the problem. It has called for the minimum sum to be raised beyond the $80,000 target, for more CPF savings to be set aside in the Special Account, and for a cap on how much can be used for property purchases. Given the state of the economy and property market, the panel struck a cautious note – who can blame them, in the dark and despondent mood on the ground at the time? – and maintained that the CPF system was sound, and that its proposals amounted to no more than a refocusing of the system to face the challenges ahead. The CPF sacred cow, in other words, was largely fine.

But does the report go far enough, or is it yet another political compromise that does not quite address the problem? Will the lower CPF contributions for workers aged 50 to 55, amounting to a saving for employers of a few hundred dollars a month, make much of a difference in making these workers employable? After all, financial planning and preparation amounts to nothing if they have no jobs. And has enough been done to ensure that what workers squirrel away is adequate for their autumnal years?

Indeed, as the panel itself notes in its report, 'As the economy grows and wages rise, successive cohorts of Singaporeans will have higher expectations of what they consider to be a basic level of needs in retirement. Over time, an annuity income of $450, based on the existing minimum sum of $80,000, will become insufficient for the majority of retirees.' The panel has called for the minimum sum to be raised beyond $80,000, but studiously avoided saying just what the new target figure should be, or what provisions should be put in place to ensure it is reached.

Furthermore, by its own reckoning, even with the proposed one-percentage-point higher contribution rates for the Special Account, about 40 per cent of CPF members will not be able to save up the minimum sum. How then is this group going to get by in retirement? How will they be provided for – and by whom?

Mr Lim's reaction to the proposals after they were announced was striking. Asked if the measures were as far-reaching as he had initially called for, he replied: 'The ERC has taken public reaction into account', adding that the changes were 'probably what the public can accept'.

Again, what the public will wear.

My worry, however, is that what the public will wear might well turn out to be a straitjacket that will hem in a future generation of Singaporeans, loading them with a heavy financial burden they might not be able to bear. Are Singaporeans aware of this? Perhaps a critical part of the problem is that many see the ageing population as something for the government to deal with. Measures to do so are viewed as initiatives that might hit their present incomes and future financial well-being, drawing howls of anguished protests.

Yet, the ageing of our society is a concern for you and me. Failure to deal with these problems will result in consequences that you and I – and our children – will have to live with. This will hit all Singaporeans below the age of 50 now, but those in their 20s and 30s especially should take note, as the future financial burden will fall largely on their shoulders.

Mr Tharman, in his reassuring way, has tried to signal this to Singaporeans, pointing to 'looming problems' that have to be tackled sooner or later. But pardon me, for I think someone had better spell it out, and refocus minds on the fact that even with the proposed changes, the CPF minimum sum is going to be scarcely enough for most people to get by. Worse, many will not even have this minimum amount in their CPF accounts. Unless this is made patently clear, some might well be lulled into complacency and imagine that the latest proposals will 'fix' the ageing problem, so that they can rely on their CPF funds for their retirement needs. They will be in for a rude shock.

So, much as the panel should be commended for a finely balanced report, I would attach on its cover a notice, which would read:

'Warning: Some users of this report might suffer from delusions, falling into a false sense of security, both about the present and the future. They might be hit by a painful hangover afterwards. Those with symptoms should see their bank managers and consult a financial adviser immediately.'

(First published 20 July 2002)

Which to save?

Moves to save the National Library, that ugly old pile of red brick, left me cold. At the height of the furore over the proposed demolition of the National Library, I marvelled at the brazen lack of interest in the fate of the nearby Cathay Building. Built in October 1939, Cathay has a real claim to being a historical building. The 17-storey 'skyscraper' was once the tallest in Southeast Asia. Yet, ironically, the building remained forlorn and dilapidated for many months without anyone seeming to notice or care, even as people were getting hot under the collar about that relatively new kid on the block, the National Library. Indeed, few tears were shed when the building was eventually demolished to make way for a modern complex.

(From 'Farewell to Taman Serasi'
14 April 2001, see page 84)

Chapter 3
Children of a simpler age

THE RISE in the cost of living hits Singaporeans squarely in their pockets. But it also strikes them hard in their hearts. For at the back of their minds are fond memories of a time not so long ago when life in Singapore was simpler, slower and cheaper. While few would give up the costly First World trappings of modern Singapore, there is a deep-seated yearning for the relatively carefree days of the past.

This battle between Singapore's globalising head and its localised heart has been raging quietly for some years now. For the most part, the tussle takes place largely beneath the surface. But the simmering sentiments emerge into the open from time to time.

This pull between going global and staying local is by no means unique to Singapore. Ask Senator John Kerry, the Democratic Party contender for the US presidency. He has been walking a tightrope, watching his flank as his rivals pandered to popular unhappiness over job losses in recent years. When rivals thundered against free trade agreements, Mr Kerry was forced to talk tough about making trade fair for Americans and his readiness to fight outsourcing of American jobs abroad, even though he has spent much of his political life as a free trader and knows full well the economic implications of doing so.

Similarly, even as President George W. Bush pushes a free market and free trade agenda, he has been careful to tend to domestic concerns about the loss of millions of manufacturing jobs to foreign firms. Significantly, on the day he signed the Free Trade Agreement with Singapore, Mr Bush made a speech declaring that the FTA was as much about opening foreign markets and generating jobs for Americans, as giving foreigners access to its markets. As the 2004 election campaign hots up, Mr Bush and his team have been busy making the right noises about the need for 'fair trade' and 'market access abroad', as well as occasionally 'bashing' China for its undervalued currency which is blamed for contributing to the trade deficit, if only to soothe domestic tempers at home. A shrewd politician, Mr Bush knows that his ability to further a free trade agenda will be undermined if the impression sticks that he is not sufficiently concerned about the woes of American workers.

In Singapore, this global versus local tension has manifested itself in several ways over the years. It was evident in the public uproar over the takeover of POSBank by DBS. Over and over again, the arguments have been repeated that the bank's old ways of operating were unsustainable, given the competition that banks here are going to face. Few would argue with this. Still, given a choice, many would have opted to stick with the popular 'People's Bank' than see it absorbed in the name of creating 'Asia's best bank'.

Whether it is in banking, or in other national icons like the Port of Singapore Authority, Singapore Airlines, Changi Airport, or right down to your neighbourhood mom-and-pop shops, the relentless imperatives of staying economically competitive is a leitmotif of Singapore politics. Boasting productivity, retraining workers, contending with new competitors, be it Malaysia or a rising China and India, have been the stuff of ministerial speeches over the years. When Singapore's leaders announce better than expected economic growth rates, they do not reach for the champagne. Instead, they start worrying how the higher growth will be sustained. Few, I think, doubt that Singapore has little choice but to adapt to the changing global economic environment – and quickly. But many are left with a lingering sense of unease about the pace and direction of change.

A similar sense of unease can also be detected in the perennial debate among young Singaporeans, which resurfaces ever so often, about just what makes Singapore stand out these days from any other cosmopolitan global city. Young Singaporeans are often the greatest champions of 'Singlish', seeing in it a way to assert their local identity, even as they hold their own, speaking the standard, internationally recognised English they had learned in schools.

Then, there is a hue and cry that inevitably follows an announcement of major public works projects that entail demolishing an old building, whether it is a ramshackle hawker centre like Taman Serasi, an ageing cinema hall such as Lido or Orchard, or a modern monstrosity such as the National Library. Don't get me wrong. I too felt sorry to see these go. But where I parted company with the conservation crowd was the knee-jerk way in which they sought to save just about every old structure from the wrecker's ball. In land-scarce Singapore, conservation needs to be more carefully considered, with advocates picking their battles, saving places and buildings that really warrant being saved for posterity. Like it or not, we simply can't save them all.

Or consider the lingering disaffection with the government's 'open door' policy, which has allowed an influx of foreign talent into the country. Recent surveys have shown that most Singaporeans view such foreign talent unfavourably, as being birds of fancy, out to enjoy the country while the going is good, only to fly off when times are tough. This aversion to foreigners has always puzzled me. After all, as a nation of immigrants, Singaporeans might be expected to be more sympathetic and welcoming towards foreigners. Indeed, if earlier generations of Singaporeans had been similarly unwelcoming, most of us would not be here on the island today.

What explains their disquiet then? At heart, I do not believe that we Singaporeans are a racist or xenophobic lot. Instead, I suspect that much of the unhappiness with the foreign talent policy stems from a sense that, while these new additions to the fold may bring skills and make valuable contributions, they also inevitably bring about changes in society here, some of which will be unwelcome.

Now, economic reform, immigration policy, and soul-searching for a national identity might seem like a mixed bag of social, political and economic concerns. But the underlying sentiment in every one of them is the same. In a way, each one is a proxy issue, reflecting a gnawing sense that the benefits that economic integration with the rest of the world brings come at a heavy social and cultural cost.

This sense of unease about globalisation is suffused with a deep nostalgia, a longing for a time when life in Singapore was simpler, slower and less stressful. Little wonder then that television programmes like *Growing Up* or *Phua Chu Kang*, and films like *Forever Fever* are so popular, for they hark back to an earlier age.

Indeed, my friendly *kopi tiam* owner in Tiong Bahru tells me that one of the bestselling soft drinks in his shop is not Coke or Pepsi but Kickapoo Joy Juice, which is still sold in its familiar green can. 'Very saleable,' he says. 'People remember it, like they do Green Spot and Sinalco. But not so easy to find those anymore.' In a similar vein, a well-known food columnist once decried government efforts to promote healthy hawker fare here, such as Hokkien mee fried without lard, declaring indignantly: 'Pork lard is my heritage!'

Government leaders, I suspect, are not unaware of these sentiments. It is perhaps for this reason that many speeches by the likes of Foreign Affairs Minister George Yeo have been peppered with references to the need to nurture the 'Singapore Spirit', while Defence Minister Teo Chee Hean talks often about the 'Singapore Heartbeat'. Their more prosaic counterparts repeat the mantra of the need to maintain social cohesion.

I can't help but wonder, though, if these go far enough. For the perception on the ground is that it is the government that is leading the charge into the new global age. And here's the rub: Followers further behind in the ranks do not always see, or understand, just where this wave of change might take them, or why they are being urged to revel in it.

Instead of having a helicopter view of the benefits of corporate synergy, higher returns on capital, or rising stock options, the man with the elf-level perspective sees only the retrenchments and redundancies, the rising unemployment rates, the widening wage gaps, the rising costs, the new technology to master, the old skills made obsolete, the old ways of life and familiar sights disappearing before his eyes.

Little wonder then that these changes give rise to apprehension, nostalgia, bewilderment, even resentment. These sentiments, which are as inevitable as change, cannot be argued away, or worse, brushed aside. In fact, change management gurus have long recognised a process they call 'grieving'. They contend that people, groups, even societies, need to 'grieve' over their 'loss', to long a little for what has been or might have been, before they can come to terms with the changes unfolding around them.

So while people might accept all the rational arguments that change is inexorable and necessary, they also yearn to know that their leaders share their sense of loss, as well as their desire to protect some of the fundamental things that they hold dear.

But government reactions to concerns about globalisation have often focused more on emphasising the inevitability and logic of the case for change. Far less attention seems to be paid to the people's need for reassurance that their concerns about preserving parts of their past will be taken to heart by the government. It is vital that they are. For at the root of these sentiments are deep-seated emotional forces of culture, identity and a sense of place. Concerns over these issues cut deep to the bone. If not well tended, they could easily be stoked and give rise to a potent political force that may be difficult to quell. That would be a great pity. For despite all the gripes, most Singaporeans would not dispute that the country has little choice but to go with the globalising tide. Ironically, Singapore cannot afford to be an island, and globalisation offers many opportunities to break out of the constraints that geography and history have imposed on it.

In the end, how far Singapore moves towards embracing globalisation will be determined by the imperatives of economic survival. But how fast it is able to do so could well depend on whether its leaders can convince the people that, while change will come, some fundamental features of society will remain pretty much the same.

When news broke in 2001 that the Taman Serasi hawker centre would be torn down, it sparked an uproar among Singaporeans. The centre, like so many other disappearing physical structures, took on a significance beyond the buildings. It reminded Singaporeans of a past when life was simpler and less stressful.

Farewell to Taman Serasi

THE NO. 1 Food Delights stall at Taman Serasi hawker centre was doing brisk business. The petite Indian woman slaved lovingly over her hot stove, making those delectable *putu piring*, round little lumps of rice flour with a touch of *gula melaka*, and some coconut on the side. She has been selling these treats since 1986, but will probably have to close when the hawkers move out at the end of October. The alternative stalls offered to her are beyond what she can afford. 'If the rent is more than $500 a month, I can't survive. How much can I make from these things?' she says with an air of resignation.

Despite it being a Tuesday afternoon, the centre is abuzz with office workers in shirt and tie, *tai tai* exchanging gossip over *teh tarik*, and a smattering of workers, taxi drivers and students tucking into various delights or just savouring the afternoon over a cuppa. They seem oblivious to the grimy red and orange tiled floor, strewn with litter, and made all the more slippery and somewhat squalid by the afternoon downpour.

I had decided to visit the place following the hullabaloo over its impending closure. It was a bit of a nostalgia trip. I had spent many an evening here during my national service days, some of which I served at the nearby Central Manpower Base in Dempsey Road. Sitting

84

there under the green shelters that blend into the canopy of ancient trees, my mind began to wander to the past, chalking up a list of other familiar places which are now, or will soon be, history.

Gone – Central Manpower Base, long since moved to Depot Road.

Gone – the old Rasa Singapura hawker centre along Tanglin Road, which we used to frequent.

Gone – my old school buildings; St Michael's School and Hwa Chong Junior College have both been rebuilt.

The old St Joseph's Institution building in Bras Basah Road, mercifully, has been saved, although works of art now hang in the classrooms as well as the little nook where my friends and I used to put together the *Josephian Newsletter*, my first foray into journalism.

The old three-room Housing Board flat where I grew up in Lorong 5, Toa Payoh, has been transformed by the HDB's Main Upgrading Programme. Almost all the old blocks around it have been torn down, and in their place new 30-storey buildings have shot up.

And soon, the squat yellow Times House building along Kim Seng Road, where I have slaved for over a decade on this newspaper, will also bite the dust, making way, perhaps, for yet another condominium project.

To be sure, each of these developments has been a step forward, a sign of progress. But the collective result is also that these familiar sights will be no more than misty memories, with no physical reminders to add solidity and distinguish them from mere daydreams.

These memories are special only insofar as they are mine. Each of you will have your own special places and moments that you recall with a glint in the eye. But it is these stories that, together, form a people's history.

But, alas, so many of these are going, going... or plain gone.

I CONFESS that I never had much sympathy for those people who are quick to protest against any move to demolish old structures. Only in Singapore, I thought, do people get overly sentimental about hawker centres or cinema halls such as the Lido and Orchard. And moves to save the National Library, that ugly old pile of red brick, left me cold.

What bothered me most was the haphazard way in which protesters rushed to oppose any move at urban renewal, only after announcements were made that some old building had to make way for development. Indeed, at the height of the hysteria over the proposed demolition of the National Library, I marvelled at the brazen lack of interest in the fate of the nearby Cathay Building. Built in October 1939, Cathay has a real claim to being a historical building. The 17-storey 'skyscraper' was once the tallest in Southeast Asia. When Japanese troops stormed Singapore, it was from this building that Radio Malaya broadcast the news. And when the British returned, it became the headquarters of the Supreme Allied Commander, Admiral Lord Louis Mountbatten. Even Lee Kuan Yew once worked there, as a translator for the Japanese. His memoirs recount a close shave in which his 'file was taken out' by the Japanese after he harboured thoughts of leaving the service.

Yet, ironically, the building remained forlorn and dilapidated for many months without anyone seeming to notice or care, even as people were getting hot under the collar about that relatively new kid on the block, the National Library.

Today, the Cathay Building is all but gone. The Preservation of Monuments Board intervened to ask Cathay Organisation to preserve at least the front podium, as part of a $100 million plan to redevelop the site, building around the façade of the old landmark. Has anybody noticed? Similarly, the old Capitol Building has been shuttered up since December 1998, despite grand plans being announced more than once by the authorities to resurrect it as a theatre.

Now, I wonder if this sad state of affairs would be the case if the government department responsible was required to pay commercial rates of rent for every month that it continued to leave the building closed and unused? Has anyone raised a hue and cry about this? Apparently no one has even noticed. But be sure that there will be a rumpus as soon as word spreads that any of these buildings is to be demolished or redeveloped.

What does this reactionary approach to conservation show? Sure, the fact that people do get upset by news of venerable old buildings being torn down is to be welcomed. Although it might make the lives of the bureaucrats involved more difficult, it shows that some people do feel passionately about wanting to preserve parts of Singapore's past for the future. I would be far more concerned if people shrugged off such news nonchalantly or with resignation.

Yet this passive conservationism does not go far enough. It is too reactive and shallow, lacking any real sense of priorities of what Singaporeans value most, and what trade-offs they are prepared to make between conserving the past and embracing the future. Too often, it is simply a case of the matter being left for the authorities to decide, and for the people to groan and gripe about their decisions afterwards. That, it seems to me, is not the best way to go about fostering a city that Singaporeans consider home, both for the past it reflects and the future it upholds.

The Urban Redevelopment Authority, I know, has made some effort to engage Singaporeans in the business of planning and projecting what the city of the future might look like, such as through its dialogues on the concept plans. Kudos also should go to it and the Singapore Tourism Board for organising an exhibition to garner feedback on its plans to make Orchard Road 'more happening'. (The plans are exciting, though they seem sadly lacking in any sense of history, apart from the perfunctory reference to the old nutmeg plantations that gave the road its name.) While many of the proposals are interesting – such as the idea to have overhead verandas – I was left with the overall impression of a designer having gone somewhat over the top in attempting to replicate a sci-fi movie set. Is there no place to remind future generations of the many historical events that took place at the Istana? Or how Wisma Atria got its name? Or the bomb blasts at Faber House? Or how the Teochews in the Ngee Ann Kongsi came to own such a huge plot of land in the area? Or what Bras Basah and Dhoby Ghaut roads were named after?

But I digress. Clearly, much scope remains for Singaporeans to be engaged in what features of the city they would like to save, and what they are prepared to give up in the name of progress. If you ask me, I would, on balance, not have opposed tearing down the old Taman Serasi hawker centre, despite my own feelings for the place. It was clearly in dire need of a major spruce-up. And besides, removing it will make way for the equally, if not more popular Botanic Gardens to expand. Like it or not, such trade-offs will have to be made.

The process of how such decisions are arrived at is as important as the choice itself. The more that Singaporeans are brought into the process and helped to understand how these decisions are reached, the better. After all, given Singapore's limited real estate, conservationists will have to pick their subjects with care.

Just as a group of civil servants formed the Garden City Action Committee to draw up a Heritage Roads Plan which gazettes selected roads that 'give Singaporeans a sense of place, and tell us where home is because they are so distinctive', there is also a need for a Heritage Building Plan. This should be the result of discussions, not just among civil servants, but other concerned citizens too.

Make haste. For as the line from the old poem goes, at my back I always hear Time's winged chariot – and the wrecker's ball – drawing near.

(First published 14 April 2001)

Young Singaporeans enjoy modern facilities such as the new Orchard cinema complex. But unless they know about the old Orchard cinema that it replaced, they risk imagining that the sleek new building had been there all along and forgetting the sweat and toil that made the new Singapore possible.

Will the good-life generation fight it out in tough times?

THE BAND SOUNDS a different beat from the one at the old Orchard cinema. A singer is belting out a new hit: 'Now I can dance... now I can dance.' A group of youngsters sways and sings along. The music resonates throughout the eight-storey Orchard Cineleisure complex, filling the fancy foodcourt, wafting through the swanky stores and rising to the new cineplex on the sixth floor. Even the giant statue of King Kong, holding up a massive screen featuring action sequences from current movies, seems to be doing a jig.

This was my first visit to the new leisure and entertainment centre, opened in 1998. It is a far cry from the Orchard cinema I remember. Mind you, I was not sad to see that old building go. I had visited it often enough, with its grand circular staircase, the sound of falling tenpins from Jackie's Bowl, the grumpy *kacang putih* man fending off the crowds who milled about the billboards. But, I had reasoned, even as Singapore preserved some of its architecturally and historically significant buildings, some of the lesser structures, such as Orchard cinema, had to go. The whole island, after all, could not be one large conservation zone.

I was not thrilled, however, by what I found in its place.

Yes, the spanking $160 million building, with its bright lights, hip music and happening people was modern, even futuristic – right down to its newfangled name. But oh, for some character and charm that might tell you that you were in Singapore, and not Seattle or Seoul.

Most of all, I was bothered that no one seemed to remember.

Surveying this happy scene, I chanced on a group of teens bantering animatedly, laughing, quite oblivious to the dark economic storm clouds looming outside. What is it that makes them happy? And what might mar this happiness, I asked, after an awkward introduction. These are strange questions to be asking on a Saturday evening, when people are more wont to seek some momentary happiness than to consider if they are happy. But the youngsters were game.

Friends, family, the familiarity of home are what make them happy, seemed to be the consensus.

And what could make them unhappy?

'Worried got no job,' ventured one, called Dennis, 16. 'Study so long, also no job, damn *cham!* (Hokkien for pathetic) How to buy house, buy car?'

'Or pay for girlfriend?' someone added, to peals of laughter.

Work, or the lack of it, the cost of living, stress or 'pressure' – the litany of familiar fears.

And did they miss the old Orchard cinema? I asked.

No, they chorused. I sighed.

STRESS, it would seem, is the number one bane of Singaporeans' lives. A 1998 *Straits Times* survey on happiness polled 458 people on what future developments in society would make them most unhappy. The chief worry was that life here might get even more stressful.

Thirty-four per cent said added stress would get them down, while 26 per cent were worried about a higher cost of living.

These two concerns were placed way ahead of society becoming less caring (16 per cent) or families here becoming less closely knit (15 per cent). And what did they worry about most? Jobs, careers, financial matters, higher cost of living, health and family, in that order.

These findings are hardly surprising, confirming those of earlier surveys. Three in four people said in a separate poll in March 1998 that Singapore is a stressful place to live in. And they pointed to the cost of living, family responsibilities and work as the top factors that caused stress.

A survey on emigration in 1997 also found that one in five Singaporeans had considered emigrating, citing the high cost of living and a stressful life as the two most common reasons for wanting to leave. Evidently, many Singaporeans wonder when the pressure-cooker environment here might cause them to go off the boil. Many also fear that the heat will be turned up over time.

Little wonder. With six in 10 of each Primary 1 cohort in future expected to be tertiary-educated, as well as the greater influx of foreign talent here, the competition for jobs, housing and cars can only intensify, so goes the argument. Given this expected trend, would talented, young and restless Singaporeans continue to make this island their home in an increasingly global world? Or will they tire of the endless rat-race and its results here – longer working hours, smaller cars, costlier homes – and seek greener pastures elsewhere?

Add to this the much lamented ageing of the population here. Would elderly Singaporeans be able to afford to live here if prices soared beyond the value of their retirement savings, which many experts say are inadequate to begin with? Would the growing seniors' lobby become a potent electoral force, able to prise ever more subsidies from the government, adding to the burden that younger workers must bear?

The mind boggles. Straight-line analyses of these trends make for gloomy and misleading forecasts. Not so long ago, after all, the conventional wisdom in the fevered property market of the early 1990s was that housing prices would rise inexorably. Buy now, save later, stretch to the maximum, was the common advice given to young couples setting up home. That is, until the economic crisis in the late 1990s pounded the foundations of this house of cards, and brought everyone back to Earth. Now, as developers and home owners watch anxiously over falling prices and returns, as once complacent workers face the threat of retrenchment, as graduates who believed they held an instant passport to the good life hunt for jobs, as yuppies chatter not just about rising share prices but also shrinking pay packets and bonuses, the folly of believing in endless upward spirals hardly needs stating. Prices will fall as surely as they will rise, and fall again, in line with the underlying economy. Boom will alternate with gloom, but neither need portend doom.

PERHAPS, I wondered in a whimsical moment, they should hold school field trips to Orchard Cineleisure, a veritable showcase of much of the cause of the stress and strain of modern-day living in Singapore.

A ticket to a movie used to cost $1.50. A packet of *kacang*, just 20 cents. A packet of the sweetened nuts, now sold by an Indian lady in a pretty sari – quite a change from the old Indian man in his dirty *dhoti* – under a yellow neon *kacang putih* sign, costs at least $1 today. I paid $7 for a ticket into the plush new cinema, with its state-of-the-art THX sound system – no, it is no longer the bowling balls you hear over the characters' voices – and soft seats, a far cry from the hard-backed wooden ones in the stalls of the old Orchard.

Afterwards, cinema-goers dine in outlets with names like Celebrities Asia, the Garfield café, or 'California Lemon, hot dog in the dip'. Alternatively, people head to one of the posh hair salons, the spa or a city club in the building.

Put simply, the old Orchard cinema and the new Orchard Cineleisure are worlds apart. The new First World standards are something Singaporeans take as a matter of course. Few, understandably, would settle for anything less, which explains why the old Orchard cinema and other dated landmarks like it had to close.

But this is not the wonder of it. What is really amazing is that the change has taken place within my short 30-year lifetime. This transformation, in scarcely over a generation, cannot but cause major stresses in a society. The shifting of gears, the setting of new sights, the endless demand for upgrading, all add up to higher cost and greater stress, which Singaporeans bemoan and yet would not have any less of. The *Straits Times* survey on stress, for example, found that most of those polled, while lamenting the pressures of modern-day Singapore, said they were coping well with it.

And few were prepared to slow down if it meant slower economic growth. Like it or loathe it, they would not trade their high-stress-high-standard-of-living to go back to the old, laid-back days. Nostalgia aside, they would pick Orchard Cineleisure over Orchard cinema any day. The upshot of this: Stress and high costs, you might say, are the karma of a small island city-state with global pretensions.

IN A WORLD of uncertainty, however, there is one sure thing: three trends – the globalisation of the world economy, the revolution in information technology, and the opening of Singapore's doors to more foreign talent – will change Singapore society dramatically in the years to come.

One aspect of the changes now being wrought by these forces has not been fully appreciated. This is the cosmopolitanisation of Singapore. You see it not just in Orchard Cineleisure, with its mix of stores with names like Phuture London, but also in the now ubiquitous Starbucks cafés, the modern answer to the *kopi tiam*. Although the Orchard is still owned by Cathay Organisation, it is the Golden Village chain that commands the local cinema scene once dominated by Cathay and Shaw. New bookstores like Books Kinokuniya and Borders have set up shop, aiming to edge out the likes of Times and MPH, if they do not adjust to take on the new challengers.

And just as foreign companies are arriving, so too are foreign talents – some 30,000 a year – made up not only of Chinese and Indians, but also others from America, Europe, South Africa and Latin America. Several hundred Frenchmen and Brazilians in Singapore, for example, watched their teams clash in the 2000 World Cup Final. These new arrivals will add a vibrancy and zest not just to Singapore's economy, but also its culture and society, changing its face in ways that can barely be imagined now.

This, plus the trend towards more Singaporeans working in the region and beyond, as companies and workers here plug into global markets, will widen horizons, raise expectations, shatter mindsets. Singaporeans, having roamed the world, will not be content to return to an old-fashioned *kampung*. They will want a global village, but with Singaporean characteristics.

In the face of these trends, can Singapore survive as a community, as an idea? Or will the combination of its internal pressures and external pulls undo it? Harvard academic Rosabeth Moss Kanter spells out this challenge for communities in a global age in her book, *World Class: Thriving Locally In The Global Economy*:

> 'Communities will need both magnets and glue. They must have magnets that attract a flow of external resources – new people or new companies – to renew and expand skills, broaden horizons and hold up a comparative mirror against world standards. ...
>
> 'Communities also need social glue – a means for social cohesion, a way to bring people together to define the common good, create joint plans and identify strategies that benefit a wide range of organisations and people in the community. ... communities also need a social infrastructure ... for collaboration to solve problems and create the future.'

Magnets and glue. Even as Singapore draws talents, investments and influences from abroad, does it have the cohesion to remain Singaporean? Will the factors that made Singapore's success possible – hard work, a determination to succeed against the odds, a commitment to multiracialism and meritocracy, the willingness of labour and management to work together, a political culture that emphasised long-term economic and social planning and organisation, and frowned on petty party wrangling – continue to hold?

An older generation, having seen the lean years, was willing to make extraordinary economic, social and even political sacrifices to make this place work. A younger generation, however, has grown up believing that the bewildering sights and sounds of the likes of Orchard Cineleisure are the natural order of things. They party in Boat Quay and at Zouk disco, quite oblivious to the fact that life for their ancestors by the wharves was no party at all.

Will they be able to hold this place together? Will they be prepared to make similar sacrifices to keep it going? Or will they take liberties with themselves, allowing their newfound affluence to lull them into forgetting that, at the end of the day, all Singapore has is barely some 660 square kilometres of land, and nothing but the wit and the will of its people to survive on?

These, to me, are the crucial questions raised – and which each generation of Singaporeans must ponder. Even in Singapore, some things don't change.

(First published 9 August 1998)

A Singaporean feat?

What do those who cast doubts over the Singapore Everest team's success in Nepal have to say about the economic Everest that this country scaled in the 1960s and 1970s, since the bulk of the Cabinet team that led us to those heights was also not Singapore born and bred? If only victories by local-born Singaporeans count, it would imply that the country's early economic progress was not a Singaporean-inspired feat. The argument is ludicrous, to say the least.

(From 'Confronting home truths on Everest'
6 June 1998, see page 107)

Chapter 4
One world, ready or not

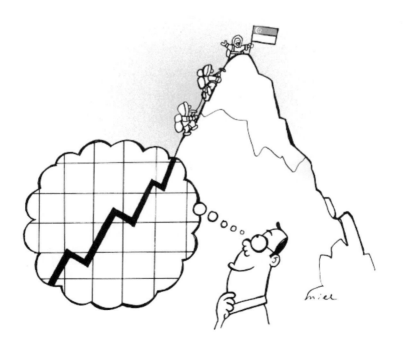

IF SOME Singaporeans look back nostalgically to a simpler age, many look ahead anxiously to the future, wondering just what it holds for them, their children and their society. Will Singaporeans be an endangered species in the age of globalisation, as a younger generation becomes more at home wandering about the world, both virtually and in real life? An undergraduate once put this question to Lee Hsien Loong at a public forum.

His hobby, the young man said, was to watch Taiwanese operas on cable television. He also spent a lot of time surfing and chatting with friends from around the world. No doubt there are many people his age who are as at home interacting with Netizens on the Web, talking about the same – mostly American – movies and the latest hits, sharing similar edgy attitudes, speaking in their familiar tongue and sounding, like, you know, so koool.

So what is it that makes them Singaporean in this global day and age? Important question. One that many more young Singaporeans of the wired generation will have to grapple with. Indeed, as Singapore continues to entice more foreigners to the country to boost its numbers, since too few babies are being born each year to replace, let alone grow the population, how will Singaporeans remain Singaporean? This begs a further question: Since most Singaporeans are themselves children of immigrants – one or two generations removed – how very different are they from the ones arriving a little later in the day? If being born in Singapore, or having had ancestors here, is a critical criterion for being a true blue Singaporean, then most of us or our parents would at one stage not have qualified. Indeed, by extension, are third generation Singaporeans more 'Singaporean' than second generation ones? The idea seems absurd. But it's a logical corollary of many of the anti-foreigner views that are common these days.

These deep-seated questions on what makes a Singaporean or makes him call this island home occupied the minds of about a dozen youngish Singaporean professionals whom I worked with on the Singapore 21 Committee several years ago. What is it about this place that would make Singaporeans feel for it, want to stay, or return to even if they could fly away for good?

The committee came up with a neat formula, as committees are wont to do. This comprised the five F's: family, friends, food, familiarity and future. A combination of these factors would make a person call Singapore home.

Mr Lee's answer to the young man made reference to most of these factors and, for good measure, suggested two other F's: fun and feeling. Singapore, he maintained, was a fun place to live in and could be even more so, accommodating the aspirations of the young and the restless. And, he added, it was also a question of feeling, of having a sense that 'here we have created a special place', where young Singaporeans have the opportunity to contribute something to keep it going.

The young man listened intently, but did not reply. I wondered, What is he thinking? Was he convinced? As he soon disappeared into the crowd, I never found out. Pity. Not least because the five F's have long been on my mind. I often mulled over them often on one of my leisurely runs along the scenic Charles River in Boston, where I spent a year in 2000. After all, even though I was in the United States, my family was never far from my thoughts. I could telephone or e-mail them whenever I felt like it for hardly any cost, since long distance phone charges had plunged. Several of them also came to visit.

I made many new friends, whose company I enjoyed. And decent Singapore food, including a mean *murtabak* and tasty chicken rice, could be had at the nearby Penang restaurant in Boston's Chinatown. Unfamiliar initially, the city's charms soon grew on my wife and me, and it came to feel like home, with little nooks that we would frequent. Boston was a fun place to be, with beautiful scenic spots just a short drive away. And with many US firms eagerly seeking recruits from the country's top universities during those heady dot.com boom times, the future did not look at all bad. I could, if I chose, sign up with one of these, as many of my classmates did.

With all the F's satisfied, what made Singapore so much more attractive that anyone might feel compelled to claim it as home? As I interacted with students from around the world, what made me 'Singaporean'?

These are, if truth be told, not easy questions to answer. In the end, it boils down to being more a matter of heart than head, an inner sense that this place is home, for better or worse. I suspect that most of my Singaporean contemporaries who were with me in Boston felt the same. In fact, some admitted that they had never felt more Singaporean than after leaving, and being away from, the country. And though we hardly knew each other before we met at Harvard's Kennedy School, there was an easy affinity among the five Singaporean families. We had similar reference points: we shared the same jokes, griped about the same things, enjoyed the same food, and perhaps even held similar hopes and fears for our collective future.

How did this happen?

The Catholics have a theory: Catch a child in his early years, implant him with a set of experiences, values and beliefs, and you have him for life. It is like anchoring him to a solid core with a strong line, long enough for him to roam the world, but to return with a 'twitch upon the thread'.

No doubt it was the early years of socialisation in Singapore schools, singing the *mari kita* daily, growing up in integrated housing estates, playing with other Singaporean children of various races, eating at hawker centres, seeing the transformation of the island before our eyes, and watching our parents and elders react to the events that shaped and shook the nation, and eventually serving in the army – all these helped imbue us with an instinctive sense of being Singaporean. It was this sentiment that ultimately drew most, if not all, of us home.

But the question remains: Will an even younger generation of Singaporeans, who are growing up in a more complex, more connected world, feel the same way?

I think so. Provided Singaporeans make the effort to pass on to a younger generation a sense of what came before, how this community pulled together, and what they must do to hold on to the idea of 'Singapore'. If nations are 'imagined communities', as some scholars have argued, then it is critical that the imagining is carried through to a new generation.

Otherwise, something very precious would have been lost. As *New York Times* columnist Thomas Friedman puts it in his book, *The Lexus And The Olive Tree: Understanding Globalisation*, 'When you strip people's homes of their distinctiveness by homogenising them, you undermine not only their culture but also social cohesion. Culture gives life structure and meaning. It sanctions a whole set of habits, behavioural restraints, expectations and traditions that pattern life and hold societies together at their core.'

No doubt, the government here is aware of this. Hence the calls from no less than Goh Chok Tong for parents to pay heed to their children, and for busy working professionals to spend time with their families. Or the exhortations for the ethnic groups to do more to mix and mingle, especially at festive times. And hence the big push to reinforce these messages through the National Education programme in schools, as well as through public rituals such as singing the national anthem and marking events like Total Defence Day.

But try as it will, the government can only do so much. In the end, it is up to you and me to teach our children well, share experiences with them, shape their values and give them a sense of who they are.

Can it be done? Will the relentless globalising tide, with its wave upon wave of technological and communications changes, make it more difficult to do so? Yes, it will, and Singapore and its people will need to adapt as they become more integrated with the world.

But to go from this to argue that being Singaporean will not be a meaningful proposition in the future is to make a logical leap that I suspect will not be borne out in practice. For powerful as the forces driving globalisation might be, they are up against an even deeper need for people and societies to find common reference points, to form bonds, establish ties and set down roots. The novelist E.M. Forster once summed up this deep human desire in a pithy phrase: Only connect.

Just as newspaper publishers and businessmen are discovering that the Internet and much trumpeted global communications revolution are not as much of a threat to their survival as they were made out to be, so too cultures and societies will survive globalisation. Indeed, I might go further and argue that the notion that globalisation will sweep up local cultures and give rise to something akin to a universal (read 'Western') norm is itself based on a myth.

Such a view is well articulated by Professor John Gray, an adviser to former British Prime Minister Margaret Thatcher, in his book, *False Dawn: The Delusions Of Global Capitalism.* His argument, put simply, goes like this: America has long been seized by the idea that its values and culture are universal. This goes back all the way to its Founding Fathers, who declared triumphantly that the truths they proclaimed were 'self evident'. In the 1980s and 1990s, this universalist credo became part of the neo-conservative agenda, with politicians asserting that America's economic lead and the modernity it gave rise to were tied to its culture, both social and political. Countries that sought the modernity that globalisation would bring would succumb to American ways and mores sooner or later, they argued.

As Gray puts it, 'The Enlightenment idea of a universal civilisation is nowhere stronger than in the United States, where it is identified with the universal acceptance of Western – that is to say, American – values and institutions. The idea that the US is a universal model has long been a feature of American civilisation... Yet, the claim of the US to be a model for the world is accepted by no other country. The costs of American economic and social success include levels of social division – of crime, incarceration, racial and ethnic conflict and family and community breakdown – that no European or Asian culture will tolerate.'

Gray goes on to add, 'The contemporary American faith that it is a universal nation implies that all humans are born American, and become anything else by accident – or error. According to this faith American values are, or will soon be, shared by all humankind. Of course, such messianic fancies are commonplace. In the nineteenth century the claim to be a universal nation was made by France, Russia and England. Now, even more than in the past, it is a perilous conceit.'

In other words, globalisation in no way heralds an end to ethnic identities, although these will evolve with time, as they always have. But in the end, people will be people. They will want to interact and connect and, in doing so, that which is immediate, local and tied to a community's collective sense of its past and sense of place, will still hold sway and have primary pull on their loyalties.

So is the Singaporean an endangered species in the age of globalisation? I doubt it. But only if we make the effort to teach and mould our children well, giving them a sense of who they are, where they came from, and where they might be headed. Then, and only then, will we be able to feel sure that they might roam the world but still return home, with a gentle twitch upon the thread.

A debate sparked in 1998 by the successful ascent up Mount Everest by a Singapore team which included permanent residents rather than citizens raised questions on just what it takes to be Singaporean, welcomed and accepted by this nation of immigrants.

Confronting home truths on Everest

SHOULD Singaporeans' joy over the success of its Everest expedition be dampened because the two men who reached the top, Edwin Siew and Khoo Swee Chiow, were Malaysian-born Singapore permanent residents? Should the country now start training a core of 'true blue Singaporeans' to be sent back so that conquering the peak might be all the more sweet, as suggested by academic Hussin Mutalib in a recent letter to the Forum page? With the Singapore Everest team – note the name – expected home tomorrow, these questions will loom large in some minds as they step into the arrival hall at Changi Airport. What would be appropriate? A heroes' welcome for successful sons of Singapore? Or just grudging praise for two passing friends who did the country a good turn?

The questions go to the heart of what it means to be Singaporean, especially in the face of the government's push to draw more foreign talent here to help the Republic scale the next peak of its economic and social development. The unease over the official red carpet for foreign talent has been latent for some time. Sure, Singaporeans recognise that these talented people are needed to give the economy a boost. Indeed, a recent survey by *The Straits Times* found that a full three in four of those polled supported the government's move to welcome foreign talent because they believed these foreigners would bring economic benefits to Singapore. But I suspect that the welcome is a lukewarm one, rather than one based on a readiness to embrace these newcomers as latter-day additions to the Singapore fold. Given a choice, Singaporeans would still prefer to rely on 'true blue Singaporeans' to achieve honours for the nation, on the sporting field or off it.

This sentiment is odd, especially in a young nation of immigrants such as this. One might ask, just what does it take to be a 'true blue Singaporean'? A pink identity card? A green reservists' booklet? A red passport? Does possession of these alone make one more patriotic and loyal? Indeed, must a Singaporean be born here? Must he live on this island throughout his life? Might the growing number of those who live and work overseas for extended periods not be considered Singaporeans? Is someone more Singaporean because two generations of his ancestors lived here, rather than one – or none for that matter? Where – and why – do you draw that crucial line? Put another way, will the children of climbers Mr Siew and Mr Khoo be more Singaporean than their fathers, both of whom have lived here for over a decade, if they happened to be born here?

What do those who cast doubts over the Singapore team's success in Nepal have to say about the economic Everest that this country scaled in the 1960s and 1970s, since the bulk of the Cabinet team that led us to those heights was also not Singapore born and bred? If only victories by local-born Singaporeans count, it would imply that the country's early economic progress was not a Singaporean-inspired feat. The argument is ludicrous, to say the least. Yet, the questions about what it means to be Singaporean are important ones, especially in this global age, where national boundaries are so readily breached by trade, travel and television. As Singapore goes regional and beyond, and more of its people work, study, live and marry overseas, what is it that will make them distinctly Singaporean? Is it the fact that they were born in KK Hospital, ate *kway teow* at Newton hawker centre, and studied at Kent Ridge? Beyond the familiar network of family and friends, what is it that will root them to Singapore, so that, as the Catholic saying goes, they might 'wander the earth but be drawn home with a twitch upon the thread'?

A Singapore 21 Committee subgroup, of which I am a member, has been discussing these issues quietly over the past few months in the comfortable confines of the Institute of Policy Studies. The Everest ascent has thrown its discussions into bold relief, making them issues for all Singaporeans to consider. To my mind, Singapore cannot but be a welcoming home for all who might seek to live, pass through or settle here, if they not only take advantage of the opportunities the place offers, but also contribute to helping it survive and thrive. What binds the newcomers and those of older vintage to this place might be that as yet still inchoate 'Singapore Idea' that Information and the Arts Minister George Yeo talked about. This is the sum of the memories of shared times past and collective visions for the future, as well as the values and principles that underpin this society.

That this young, fragile nation is still grappling with what, and who, might subscribe to this charmed circle is perhaps not all that surprising. The questions will remain with us for years. Indeed, even a relatively older country like the United States is struggling with them today, as the on-going debate in the US Congress on how many foreign engineers should be allowed into the country shows. Last month, after much debate, the Senate passed a Bill to nearly double the annual cap on the number of skilled foreigners allowed into the United States, to 115,000 by the year 2000, from the present ceiling of 65,000 a year. This year's limit has already been hit, causing labour shortages in Silicon Valley, where talent from India and China has been helping to keep American firms at the top of the innovation table.

In a commentary on the debate in the *New York Times* in April, columnist Thomas Friedman quoted T.J. Rodgers, founder of Cypress Semiconductor, as saying: 'For every foreign engineer you let me bring into this country and put to work at Cypress, I will guarantee you five new jobs locally to make a microchip, sell the chip, ship the chip, market the chip and administrate the chip. The winners and losers in the information age will be differentiated by brainpower. Four out of my 10 vice-presidents are immigrants. Some 35 per cent of my engineers are immigrants. The guy who designs my most advanced chips – he is from Cuba. If I could hire all the engineers I need locally, I'd love to do it. But I can't. They're just not here. So if we don't bring them here, they will still be engineers in their home countries, only instead of working for us they will be working for Hitachi or Samsung, and they will compete with us from overseas and take away our wealth.'

Sound familiar? Mr Friedman concluded with this question: 'Would you like the jobs in your country depending on only the engineers your country could produce, or would you like to have access to the top 10 per cent of all engineers in the world?'

Now, if the United States, with its 250 million people from sea to shining sea, should see the wisdom of drawing talent from around the world, making them feel at home and assimilating many of them, to help it stay in the premier league of nations, what makes anyone in tiny Singapore imagine we can go the other way?

(First published 6 June 1998)

The debate over the ageing of society and immigration of foreigners to make up for the falling population has raged in Singapore in recent years, just as it has abroad. When two Nanyang Technological University academics published a study in August 2003 to argue that the government's open door policies on immigration benefits foreigners more than Singaporeans, they drew a sharp response from Acting Manpower Minister Ng Eng Hen. He dismissed the notion, arguing that it would be foolhardy for any elected government to act against Singaporeans' interests, since they – and not foreigners – are its voters to whom leaders are accountable.

No running away from global race to woo talent

TWENTY-THREE-YEAR-OLD MP Philipp Missfelder caused a rumpus in Germany recently when he declared that 85-year-old people should not expect youngsters to pay for their hip replacements. 'People used to just use crutches,' he cried, lamenting that his generation was being saddled with the mounting bill for medical treatment for the elderly. An incensed member of his own Christian Union party shot back: 'If he were my grandson, I'd spank him.'

Having paid into the state health care and pension system for years, older voters in Germany are not inclined to listen to the cry of Mr Missfelder and his generation. It's payback time. But, despite the uproar, most people know that the young MP was not speaking nonsense. After all, Germany, like many other developed societies, is ageing – rapidly. A study by the Brookings Institute has found that in about 50 years, the average age in Europe would have shot up to 52.3 years, from 37.7 now. In contrast, the average age in the United States will be 35.4 years, only slightly higher than at present. By 2050, the ratio of German contributors to the pension system to those drawing from it will fall to 2:1, from the present 4:1.

The solution, as everyone who studies the issue knows, is not only to retune the system of benefits and payments, but, more importantly, to draw in more young people to help keep the system going. The same trends apply in Japan. By 2050, Japan will have 30 per cent fewer people and a staggering one million 100-year-olds, the *New York Times* reported recently. The shrinking population will mean fewer workers, falling demand, and a 'potential collapse of the pension system as the tax base shrinks and the elderly population booms'. A recent United Nations report noted that Japan needs as many as 17 million new immigrants by 2050 to address its people shortfall. If this happened, foreigners would make up 18 per cent of the population, a leap from the present one per cent. Notoriously averse to foreigners, Japan has absorbed just one million people from abroad in the past 25 years.

Little wonder then that Japanese population expert Hiroshi Komai was quoted by the *NYT* as saying, 'Societies have always risen and faded, and Japan will likely disappear and something else will take its place, but that's not such a problem. Greece and Rome disappeared too.'

In both Germany and Japan, the solution – namely, immigration – is itself a major political problem, sparking fears among the local population about foreigners taking their jobs and changing their societies. Even in the Czech Republic, traditionally a net exporter of people, the government stoked controversy when it recently launched a 'foreign talent' drive to woo skilled workers abroad, in the face of a 10 per cent unemployment rate at home.

The situation is little different from that in Singapore, where MPs quizzed Acting Manpower Minister Ng Eng Hen on Thursday on the issue of whether jobs that are being created were benefiting Singaporeans or foreigners more. As in Germany and Japan, society here is being hit by the double whammy of rapid ageing and plunging birth rates, causing dependency ratios to turn unfavourably against the young. Even if Singaporeans start 'copulating like mad' (to borrow the inimitable phrase once used by former Cabinet minister S. Rajaratnam), they are going to have to make up the numbers by drawing more people here, like it or not.

Whatever one makes of the recent dispute over the number of jobs which go to locals or foreigners, let's face it, the underlying reason the figures have caused such a stir here is no different from that in Germany, Japan or the Czech Republic – an aversion to a flood of foreigners, often viewed as 'them' and not quite 'us'. I have always found this view very odd for a young society of immigrants like Singapore, where almost everyone is a son or daughter of an immigrant, once or twice removed. If our grandparents had held similar 'keep them out of my turf' views, many of us might not even be here having this debate.

But there's just no wishing away this anti-foreigner sentiment on the ground here or abroad, which governments everywhere have to manage. Perhaps this explains the government's attempt to put a quick end to the debate through a 'robust response' to the academics whose numbers it queried on the very day they were published. It has done no good. Instead, it simply reinforced the misguided impression that the foreign talent debate is something peculiar to Singapore, with policies here being more favourable to foreigners than elsewhere. On Thursday, Dr Ng attempted to correct this perception, arguing that simply turning away foreigners would not mean more jobs for Singaporeans.

Yet, such a view takes in only half the picture. Foreigners don't just take up jobs, they also create them. Every new foreign worker needs a home, and provides work for property agents, house movers and decorators. Workers, local or foreign, eat, have their hair cut or go to the movies, generating demand for all these services, and therefore jobs for people here. So having more foreigners come here is not an unmitigated disaster for local workers.

Indeed, a survey on immigration into London, published in the latest issue of the British magazine, *The Economist*, makes this plain. It noted that the number of work permits issued rose from about 30,000 a year in the mid-1990s to 137,500 last year – under a Labour government at that. Permits were issued especially for the kinds of workers who are in short supply everywhere – IT professionals, nurses, doctors, among others.

'What has this done for Britain?' the magazine wondered. 'Changed London dramatically, for a start. When did you last have a British waiter? When did you last go to a City reception and not hear a mix of accents? Can you imagine the blandness of the place without them?'

The influx of people into London, the report added, has boosted property prices (a boon for homeowners), created demand for services and caused London's economy to grow more rapidly than that of the rest of the country. And as some people moved out of the capital to avoid the crowds, they helped spark a revival and redevelopment of some areas in the suburbs.

The magazine concluded: 'Immigration may be politically sensitive, but the government understands how migration has driven London's economy and London has driven Britain's. It wants the motor to keep on running... Immigration is changing Britain, and people find change frightening. Governments need to be careful. But the best thing for Britons to do about immigration would be to embrace it. It is nice to be wanted. And, economics aside, foreigners make the place infinitely more fun.'

The interesting thing is this: Replace London and Britain with Singapore in the above statements, and the arguments would be just as sound. Ultimately, getting Singapore's foreign talent policy right, and making the changes needed in society to entice talented young people here, will make all the difference to whether this place continues to thrive in the future, or falls instead into a grey, dull, sullen, old age.

Given the global race to woo talent, Singapore has precious little choice but to join in. It can hardly afford to be grudging or coy about it. Instead, it would do well to remember the words of that old Cole Porter song: 'Birds do it, bees do it, even lazy jellyfish do it... Let's do it.'

(First published 16 August 2003)

As the world around them convulses in turmoil and terror, some young Singaporeans choose to remain cocooned from it all, and cynical, even dismissive of current affairs at home and abroad. But does this blissful ignorance about the ways and goings-on in the world bode well for their future?

Gen M: Are you world-ready?

OYAN embraced me with tears in her eyes. She was the wife of a friend, Eddie, who spent a year with me at graduate school in 2000. I ran into her again in October that year, a few months after we graduated, after a talk on leadership by Senior Minister Lee Kuan Yew at Harvard University.

'You are so lucky,' she said, clearly emotional. 'If only my country could also have good leaders.'

This was no mere platitude. Oyan and Eddie had put their lives on the frontline of the movement to oust Filipino dictator Ferdinand Marcos in the 1980s. Eddie had given up the comforts of a life as a provincial doctor to run for the mayorship of his area, standing against the 'guns, girls and goons' of a corrupt incumbent. Oyan had been jailed for her activism in non-government organisations, leaving her husband to look after their children, even as he fought for her release.

Later, they both campaigned to deny President Fidel Ramos another term, thinking that it was better to stick with constitutional principle than simply back a good man. They, therefore, watched with horror last year as their country slid deeper into corruption, cronyism and chaos under Joseph Estrada, who stepped into the political void left by the departing Mr Ramos.

'We were naïve. We should have kept Ramos,' she once told me, her voice heavy with resignation.

As I watched events unfold in Manila in April 2001, as Vice President Gloria Arroyo moved to unseat and replace Mr Estrada, I could not help but recall the despair in Oyan's eyes, and wonder what she would make of the 'state of rebellion' that had been imposed on her forlorn country. Given the way the new President had been swept into office, through defections of generals and politicians rather than any democratic process, it was perhaps to be expected, despite all the democratic pretensions of People's Power II.

Meanwhile, not far away, in an undeclared state of rebellion, then Indonesian President Abdurrahman Wahid was fighting similarly for his political life. To the north, both Malaysia and Thailand also had leaders struggling to shore up their positions, whether in the courts or on the ground.

Further afield, a new US President George W. Bush was finding his way in the world of geopolitics, bumbling and brushing against sentiments in China, Russia and Europe in the process. In Japan, the new Koizumi administration had been installed and many are watching to see whether it can help the country break out of its decade-long economic malaise.

Against this backdrop, who can say that these are not 'interesting times'? These events are anything but boring, and how they shape up could have a bearing on our lives for many years to come.

But, cut to safe, serene Singapore, and what do you find? A new Generation M (Millennium) – edgy, cynical, globally connected, and blissfully oblivious of the world around them, both at home and abroad. If a portrait of the lives of well-educated and well-heeled teens – born in the last millennium but growing up in this one – published in *The Straits Times* that week in April 2001 was anything to go by, these youngsters spent most of their time buried in their books, hanging out at upmarket coffeeshops and yakking on their mobile phones when they were not using them to send endless SMS messages to each other.

They remind me of the lines from that great Paul Simon song, *Born At The Right Time*: 'Never been lonely, never been lied to, never had to scuffle with fear, nothing denied to …'

Born with a silver spoon in their mouth, as Goh Chok Tong (who coined the term Gen M) put it, they believe that to be cynical is to be cool. To be anti-Establishment is de rigueur. To be hip is to be holier-than-thou, never deigning to show any sign of interest in the mundane matters of the day, let alone getting involved in them. Politics is propaganda, history lessons are brainwashing sessions. Current affairs? Boring, don't waste my time. Opinions? Nah, the system drummed it out of us. Participation? Please, where's the time?

Such cynicism is cheap. Apathy is so simple – it is always somebody else's role, somebody else's fault, somebody else's business. Wired and connected, Gen M-ers say they want to see the big, wide world, to travel, work and live there, if only to get away from 'small, restricted Singapore'. Yet, their idea of the world out there seems more virtual than real, centred on images of the developed West, of cities rather than countryside, and myths about a technologically and socially advanced one-world, where all men are equal, educated, ethnically neutral and with similar edgy views about life, labour and love.

No doubt, these young minds will grow and mature, with time and exposure to the world. Travel, they say, broadens minds. Besides, every generation laments the follies and foibles of the next. Yet, I cannot help but fear that not a few of them are headed for a fall, a shock to their senses, a shattering of their get-rich-quick, retire-at-40 dot.com dreams.

This sense of unease about whether Gen M is growing up in virtual reality is well captured in *Global Soul: Jet Lag, Shopping Malls And The Search For Home*, by travel writer Pico Iyer. In his book he notes,

> 'The richest 358 people in the world, by United Nations calculations, have a financial worth as great as that of 2.3 billion others and, even in the United States, the prosperous home of egalitarianism, the most wired man in the land, Bill Gates, has a net worth larger than that of 40 per cent of the country's households, or perhaps 100 million of his compatriots combined.
>
> 'The rich have the sense that they can go anywhere tomorrow, while 95 per cent of the new beings on the planet are among the poor; I worry about the effects of e-mail and transprovincialism, while two-thirds of the world have never used a telephone.'

To bring home his point, Iyer takes his readers to Haiti, just two hours from New York City.

> 'Stepping off the plane, I walked into the pages of the Bible. Women were relieving themselves on the main street, and the principal sights on view along National Highway One were tombstones ... Most of the adults I saw around me, I learnt,

had never had a day of formal schooling, and the average man would be dead by the age of 44.

'Haiti still remains the globe's rule rather than exception – more and more countries I visit are descending into anarchy … There are more telephones in Tokyo, it is often said, than on the entire continent of Africa. But these very discrepancies are one of the by-products of the age, and more and more of us, moving between countries as easily as between channels on our screen, are tempted to underestimate the distances between them.'

The point here is this: Unless our Gen M-ers understand how this country got where it is, how it relates to the region around it, as well as the wider goings-on in the world, they will never have the 'Big Singapore' mindset that Trade and Industry Minister George Yeo talks about. Without it, equipped with only a superficial sense of globalism, they will be focused too narrowly on themselves and their seemingly pressing woes to see or understand the many opportunities open to them.

Gen M-ers may be au fait with Hollywood. But do they know about Haiti and Hanoi? They may dream of making it big in Manhattan. But do they know about the nightmares of people in Manila or the plight of the Madurese?

They may think that not having a mobile phone is a 'social handicap'. Do they know that this island is more wired than many countries, or how or why this is possible? They may moan and groan about how dull this place is. Do they know about the 'excitement' breaking out in countries all around them? They may think these events are far off and removed from their charmed lives and will probably never affect them because Singapore is, well, different. Do they know how it became so, or what they must do to keep it that way?

Oh, how boring! they might cry. For their sakes, and that of this country, you and I have a role to play in making sure they find out, sooner rather than later. Sure, perhaps the National Education classes launched in 1997, to try to help them find answers to some of these questions, could be improved. Perhaps the methods of delivery might be subtler, slicker, given more spin, made more interactive and even more fun.

All that is well and good. But let's not kid ourselves, or our children for that matter. Let's not let them grow up with the notion that history can be sugarcoated or jazzed up. That political realities can be wished away or ignored into oblivion. Or that the rights and responsibilities of citizens are anything to be sniffed at or be cynical about. Or that gaining an understanding of the world will be possible without putting in more time and painstaking effort than simply surfing the Net, while slurping up another cafe latte.

(First published 5 May 2001)

In the new globalised world, some Singaporeans will choose to live and work abroad. That is fine, so long as they do so with their eyes open. Some, however, put on rose-tinted glasses. They paint an idealised world out there, where life is beautiful, and contrast it with a life of drudgery back home. Not only is this misleading, it's needlessly dispiriting for the young back home, who should be challenged not to quit on their society, but instead stay and reshape it as they would like it to be. The following column was sparked by the 'stayer or quitter' debate that arose from a speech by Goh Chok Tong in August 2002.

Stayer, quitter, dreamer, planner – which will it be?

A BRIGHT, young friend sent me an e-mail which read: 'Young adult Singaporeans are really pissed off at the whole stayer/quitter thing. Many, many people are quite upset.' It came attached with a copy of an old article by Colin and Joycelyn Goh, titled 'Paved with good intentions'. Just about everyone she knew had read and was talking about this posting on the Net. It painted a picture of the relentless quest for the Singapore Dream of the five C's, and lamented how this had unwittingly become a Singapore Plan, in which many adults found themselves trapped. 'All think it is amazingly accurate in describing Singapore,' was how my friend summed up the reactions of her peers.

I recognised the name, Colin Goh, of Talkingcock.com fame. I had met him one cold, wintry morning in February 2000 in Philadelphia, when we both addressed a group of Singaporeans who were studying in the United States. A charming, engaging speaker, Colin was a hit with the audience. He told his story, of how he had decided to pack up and leave for New York to pursue his dreams of being an artist and an entrepreneur, rather than trodding the path most followed, of taking a scholarship and then chasing career, car and condo. In Singapore, people listened too much to that familiar inner voice, which declared, '*Ling peh gong ...*' (Hokkien for 'Your father says'), followed by no end of injunctions on what to do, and just how to do it, on virtually every aspect of their lives. Obediently, they followed the old man's plan.

Colin's remarks resonated with the young people present. He spoke to them and, in a way, for them. His article repeats his story and message. After a colourful description of how they had made the decision to head for New York, his wife, Joycelyn, puts two scenarios to readers:

'Consider these two stories. Which is closer to yours? You wake up every day and work from Monday to Friday, and often Saturday too. If you finish work early, you and your partner go to your parents' place for dinner and see your children for a few hours. If you work late, you buy a packet of *char kway teow* from the hawker centre... You're not crazy about your job but you know that if you keep it, you can afford a car in three years' time and, in five years' time, buy a condo. Your conversations with people are either for the purpose of networking, work or for familial obligations you cannot avoid. On weekends, you play golf with your friends at your country club or watch a movie with your partner. Once a year, you go on a 10-day vacation to New York, London or Paris.

'Alternatively, you wake up and you have no idea what is going to happen today, tomorrow, six months or a year later. Ironically, because of this uncertainty, all possibilities exist for you. You can be the prime minister of Singapore, you can make a movie, you can cook a meal you have never cooked before ... you can skip instead of walk. You have conversations with people who set your heart palpitating and your mind on fire. Your weekday is no different from your weekend because every day you are thinking, creating and, more important, imagining.

'Most of us recognise the first story and its pursuit of the five C's of cash, condo, car, country club and credit card. It is the Plan, which imposes a conclusion on you, and you work in order to make all the pieces fit... A Dream, on the other hand, carries you on its wings to worlds that your heart and mind have never known.'

Taking up the narrative, Colin adds that the Singapore Plan was the result of the prevailing social ideology that was imposed on the people. He admits, though, that he was 'complicit in my unhappiness', by not being questioning enough to reject the Plan. It is heady stuff, and hardly surprising that the passion with which he delivers his iconoclastic message strikes a chord with his readers.

Yet, my problem with 'Paved with good intentions' is that for all its good intentions of wanting to challenge the young to think for themselves, it does not quite tell the whole story or go far enough. Indeed, by framing his message as a simple dichotomy between a dream-like New York and a drudgery-filled Singapore, he risks readers missing the point.

To my mind, this Dream versus Plan divide is both as helpful and confusing as the over-simplification behind the 'stayers versus quitters' one. In a sense, the debate on whether people who leave Singapore are quitters is old hat. For me, it became passé the day – some time in the 1990s, I remember covering the event – Senior Minister Lee Kuan Yew stood up before a crowd of Singaporeans living in Australia and told them how his younger Cabinet colleagues had persuaded him to change his views about people like them. Whereas he used to view them somewhat negatively, he now saw them as part of the Singapore diaspora, with something to contribute to the country, and not just economically.

I doubt very much that Goh Chok Tong, years down the road, would want to revive this sterile debate on whether people who leave the country are loyal citizens or traitors. Instead, he went on to add that more needed to be done to give Singaporeans a stake in the country, not just a material sense of belonging, but also emotional and psychological bonds to the place. The Remaking Singapore Committee, chaired by Minister of State Vivian Balakrishnan and of which I was a member, did just that, proposing several ideas to strengthen ties to the country. It also spent months engaging young Singaporeans on the future they want, challenging them to rise beyond the five C's. Together, they went about imagining a society which goes beyond the Singapore Plan, where there are alternative definitions of success, many career paths and options, as well as opportunities for people to chase their disparate dreams.

In this new Singapore, you won't need to go to New York to be an artist or entrepreneur. Nor need you feel pressured into studying law or medicine if you do not want to.

But talk is cheap. The real question is whether young Singaporeans will be able to seize the day and make it happen. In the end, it is really up to them, the choices they make and the actions they take.

Don't like your job? Change it. Unhappy about the long hours at work? Change or work around it. Want to do more with your leisure rather than just watch movies or play golf? Go ahead and do so. Nobody says it will be easy. But I simply cannot buy the view that Singaporeans are mindless players blown about by circumstance.

Will young Singaporeans take up this challenge? Or will they say, as Colin writes in his article, that 'my parents never forced me into doing law. I just read their minds, I guess. Besides, all my friends were doing it. It was the Singapore Dream.'

Will they argue that it was some external ideology, the system, peer pressure, or the government, that compelled them to do as they did not want to do, think as they did not want to think or feel as they did not want to feel? Will they lament that nothing would ever change in Singapore, or say that making the change was up to the government, or that they were too afraid to 'fight for what they believe in', as Colin puts it?

That, to me, would be the ultimate sign of 'quitting', intellectually, emotionally and psychologically, even if they stayed physically in Singapore. What is worse, they would have quit not just on Singapore, but themselves, and even on life itself. That would be the pity of it all. For whether you are in New York or Newton, Boston or Bedok, London or Leng Kee, life is what you make of it.

To my mind, the significance of Mr Goh's 'stayers versus quitters' challenge was thus to ask a younger generation if they would rise or shrink from the task of remaking the country in ways they say they want, and make it work and thrive, as their forefathers had done. Would they stay the course and pursue the dream even when the inevitable setbacks arise, or would they quit and simply say it was all someone else's fault, someone else's responsibility?

So, tell me, which will it be? Stayers or quitters, dreamers or planners – the future is in your hands.

(First published 31 August 2002)

What's your channel?

More discussion may help Singaporeans appreciate the views on other ethnic or social groups, or 'channels', but this does not mean that before long, everyone here is likely to be followers of the same political programmes. A plural society will always have groups that see issues from different perspectives. So long as there is a broad consensus among all Singaporeans on the major issues, it will not matter unduly that they tune in to different channels. Trying to create a one-view, one-channel Singapore is likely to lead to less pleasant viewing all round.

(From 'Are Singaporeans on different political wavelengths?'
25 July 1991, see page 142)

Chapter 5
One nation, one people, one Singapore?

'We, the citizens of Singapore, pledge ourselves as one united people, regardless of race, language or religion...'

We recited these words every morning. In neat rows, dressed in our school uniforms, we stood before the Singapore flag, mouthing the words without really thinking what they might mean. It did not matter. Multiracialism, after all, was part and parcel of our lives – in the classroom, on the playing field and in the Housing Board estate where I grew up. The old, deep divides of race, language and religion that our society has long had to grapple with never quite impinged on our youthful consciousness.

I recall Mohan, one of my closest friends in primary school, with whom I did just about everything. From struggling with homework, to playing soccer before school and during recess, and stumbling upon the birds and the bees. It never occurred to me to ask if he was Hindu or Muslim. It did not matter. We were just two kids, growing up and mucking around.

So it was with the neighbourhood friends I made. A group of us formed a soccer team, with Malays, Chinese and Indians. We trained every weekend to take on other teams. We lost many games, but we had fun together on and off the pitch. My Chinese neighbours often took me to the Kong Chian cinema in Toa Payoh Central to watch Mandarin movies – from Bruce Lee to Agnes Chen – and unwittingly laid the foundation for my study of the language when I went to school. Eventually, I ended up at Hwa Chong Junior College, but I did not find its Chinese ethos alien or unwelcoming, contrary to the popular stereotype of the college at that time.

For years as a boy, I was a member of the famous Peter Low choir, which sang at the Risen Christ Church in Toa Payoh. When the choir embarked on a goodwill tour of the United States, I happily donned a yellow and gold *baju, sarung* and *songkok*, while others in the group put on Chinese and Indian costumes to showcase Singapore's ethnic diversity before American audiences. But alas, try as hard as I might, I just could not do a decent *joget*, unlike some of my more agile peers!

My parents never objected to me coming and going with my neighbours and friends, visiting their homes, sometimes sharing their meals and occasionally bringing goodies home. So, in my heart and in my mind, I am nothing if not Singaporean. My father was Indian, my mother, Eurasian, my wife, Chinese. But none of these ethnic labels fits me as comfortably as being called Singaporean.

I do not think that my experiences growing up in independent Singapore are unique. Many others in their 30s, 40s and beyond have told me that they, too, recall a largely 'race-blind' childhood. Many, however, also lament that people are becoming more race-conscious these days. This strikes me as ironic: How is it that a generation which came of age in a multiracial milieu is now bringing up children who are more aware of ethnic divides?

What are we to make of the stories of parents telling their children 'not to mix with those of other races and religions', or not wanting their children in certain schools where another race is predominant? Or of reports of students breaking up into segregated groups outside the classroom?

Each time these concerns flare up, fingers are immediately pointed at the usual suspects in the ethnicity debate – race-based self-help groups, Special Assistance Plan schools and the Speak Mandarin campaign – as causes that have led to the races moving further apart rather than being drawn together. To be sure, these policies have contributed to a rise in ethnic consciousness. Each of these initiatives might be justified not only for the specific goals they were meant to achieve, but also for the larger one of helping the various ethnic groups here to anchor themselves and deepen their own cultural roots in the face of the global cultural onslaught from the West. A laissez-faire approach to culture and ethnicity would not necessarily have produced a more 'Singaporean' Singapore but, perhaps, an even more culturally confused pseudo-Westernised one. Few, I think, want that.

But perhaps the sum of the parts of these policies is greater than the whole. So even if you accept that ethnic self-help groups are more effective in reaching out to their respective communities and addressing their specific problems, it might be asked if ways cannot be found for these groups to work more closely under an umbrella body to tackle common concerns, such as educational underachievement or problems with youth gangs, which exist in segments of all the communities. Might not more be done to ensure greater racial diversity in schools here, not just in the SAP schools, but also in some neighbourhood schools?

One of the schools that fell unwittingly under the media glare in January 2002 for having a *tudung*-wearing student, revealed that 57 per cent of its students were Malay/Muslims. That's one in two of all students at the school, a surprising figure in a country that has placed ethnic quotas to ensure racial integration in public housing estates. Is that healthy or wise?

One idea that was taken up by the Remaking Singapore Committee, of which I was a member, was for the need to do more to assert the 'Singaporean-ness' of Singapore, even as we seek to promote and preserve the component cultures that make up our society. Efforts need to be made to ensure that the disparate ethnic strands, even while celebrating their diversity, cohere into a solid whole.

A practical measure, unveiled after the arrests of a group of Jemaah Islamiah terrorists in 2001, was for the setting up of Inter-Racial Confidence Circles (IRCC), new grassroots groups that will bring the leaders of various ethnic bodies together and make it easier to discuss and resolve sensitive ethnic issues whenever they crop up. At first blush, the idea of yet another government-led civic group might not be attractive. But given that society here has become more settled, and people have fallen quite naturally into their own social circles, mere hand-wringing over the problem will not do. Forging closer ties will call for some conscious effort and, in this regard, the IRCCs are as good a place to start as any.

Yet, simply adding another 'C' to the veritable alphabet soup of community groups, such as the RCs and CCCs and CCMCs (now honestly, how many know what all these stand for or do?), will not be enough to achieve the ties that bind that we are now seeking. Let's face it; these administrative solutions will only go so far. While the government should take the lead, the push for greater social integration among the races here will not be effective unless Singaporeans themselves embrace the idea of multiracialism and are prepared to live the ideal. After all, multiracialism cannot be an 'extracurricular activity'. It is something that Singaporeans – you and I – will have to put into practice in our daily lives if the quest for stronger bonds across races is going to be more than a slogan bandied about on Racial Harmony Day. Interracial activities cannot be held just for community groups to tote up impressive statistics for their political masters. Otherwise cynicism will soon set in and the multiracial ideal that this country was founded on will be debased, reduced to just so many empty words that kids parrot on the school grounds.

More perhaps needs to be done to celebrate the multiracial ideal that gave birth to Singapore. Efforts are being made through the National Education programme in schools. But to bring the message home, politicians, parents, teachers and just about everyone else have a role to play in conveying to our young the stories that lie behind the making of multiracial Singapore. Yes, tell them a story. Tell them about how Singapore came to be expelled from Malaysia because of the multiracial ideal that its leaders espoused. Tell them how having independence thrust upon Singapore was not greeted with whoops of joy, but a real sense of foreboding because it was plain to all that living up to the ideal would never be easy.

Indeed, bridging the age-old divides of race, language and religion calls for sustained, painstaking efforts all round, with much accommodation, compromise and give-and-take from all sides. It has always been so and remains the case today, especially given the heightened ethnic and religious fervour in some quarters.

Consider these examples: Some Muslims nowadays are less willing to join non-Muslim friends for meals. It used to be only that pork and alcohol should not be served to Muslims at such occasions. Now, it is more common to find some asking for separate tables and even that the restaurant itself be certified *halal*. Some go so far as to demand that even the non-Muslims not eat pork or consume alcohol. The upshot: Muslims, by choice, end up cutting themselves off from the mainstream by not being willing to give and take to make a multiracial occasion feasible. Everyone ends up the poorer for it.

Another real-life example: Muslim workers in an office here have taken to broadcasting their prayer music over their radios, even as other workers are busy going about their duties. While most workers may choose to 'close an eye and an ear', this begs the question of how any work would get done if Christians started playing Gregorian chants and Buddhists began chanting mantras at the workplace as well.

Some Muslim friends of mine took umbrage at this view, when I first voiced it in a Thinking Aloud column. How, they wondered, could I ask Muslims to make accommodations for the sake of racial integration? My reply is simple: All Singaporeans need to recognise that the multiracial setting they live in sometimes calls for a bit of give-and-take, knowing when to assert your rights, and when it might be better to accommodate the feelings and concerns of others in the community.

Let me be clear: this need for mutual accommodation does not apply only to one community. I would object to, say, Catholics insisting that no meat be served at company dinners on Fridays just because some of them choose not to consume it then. Similarly, I am against the practice of some overzealous Christians, who visit hospitals trying to convert patients on their sickbeds, a time when they are most vulnerable spiritually. A well-educated Indian friend of mine once lamented that it still rankles to this day, each time she recalls how the Chinese parents of her classmates used to tell their children that Indians like her were 'black', 'smelly' and 'no good'. Then, there is the longstanding complaint among minority group Singaporeans about the tendency of some Chinese-speaking colleagues to break into Mandarin even when they are in ethnically diverse groups, leaving some members in the dark as to what, or who, is being talked about.

Little things, trifling things. But big problems loom unless Singaporeans of all races are conscious of them, and make the effort to reach out in small and practical ways, not just to smooth over ethnic encounters but also to genuinely bridge the ethnic divide. No state organisation, administrative fiat or political lecture will suffice to open hearts and minds and do the work that is needed to foster ties that bind. It will take goodwill, relentless effort and much give-and-take on all sides, from the likes of you and me, if the multiracialism that gave rise to this country and espoused in our national pledge – 'we, the citizens of Singapore' – is to remain meaningful and alive.

A longstanding debate has raged about the pursuit of a 'Singaporean Singapore', where the common theme of being Singaporean would help pull ethnically diverse peoples together. I waded unwittingly into this minefield in my very first column on 26 August 1990. It was little more than a week after I had joined The Straits Times after graduating from Oxford. Having been away from the country for three years, I was oblivious of the passions that the debate had stirred. The debate continues to this day.

A great little nation?
Start by being Singaporeans first

RETURNING to Singapore on the eve of National Day in 1990, after three years abroad, was a thought-provoking experience. The talk of the town had passed from the gloomy recession of the 1980s to more upbeat banter of national rejoicing, of building a 'great little nation'.

A great little nation? To be sure, Singapore already has most of the trappings of a major – yes, even a great – city. A tutor of mine at Oxford, for example, used to say, only half in jest, that whenever he travelled between London's Heathrow and our Changi Airport, he was at a loss as to which was the developed and which the developing country. And our spectacular 25th birthday celebrations were comparable to the extravaganza I attended in Paris in 1989 to mark the 200th anniversary of the French Revolution.

But a great little nation? Now that is a tall order, even by Singapore's demanding standards. For while we might wish to inculcate a sense of nationhood in our people, it is not something they can be taught or trained in. Passion, if you like, requires spontaneity.

I watched then, with not inconsiderable interest, as Singaporeans tunefully declared themselves *One People, One Nation, One Singapore*. In spite of the obvious popularity of these songs, I could not help feeling that something was amiss. Incessantly telling a man to *Stand Up For Singapore* may, at best, leave him with a sense that he ought to be patriotic. But it does not go far enough towards giving him a sense of why he should be so, or make him want to be so. A second generation of songs that provide vignettes of Singapore and its unique way of life will, I believe, strike a deeper chord. For example, the American patriotic song, *America The Beautiful*, which extols the natural glory of their continent 'from sea to shining sea', with its 'amber waves of grain' and 'purple mountain majesty', never fails to stir an American audience.

Being a nation also entails a sense of common identity and shared values. While it would have been naïve to expect the emergence of a Singaporean identity in such a short time, I always imagined that we had passed the stage of being 'a hotchpotch of wary ethnic strangers', to borrow the words of S. Rajaratnam in a speech earlier this year. But the long-running debate over Group Representation Constituencies, Malays in the SAF, the racial balance in Singapore and in our HDB estates, have all resulted in a palpable rise in ethnic sensitivity. In a healthy democracy, such issues should be debated openly and rationally. Yet we seemed over the years to have developed a unique style for handling such 'sensitive' issues.

Race has long been discussed in the context of the overriding principle of 'Singaporean first'. So while we would all want Singaporeans to be more aware of their ethnic origins, this should serve to enrich that unique blend that is Singapore. For while some might contend that a simple melting-pot brew to pressure-cook a Singapore identity would be unpalatable, I think most Singaporeans would still pick a multiracial recipe for a Singaporean Singapore.

The issue of race in Singapore is then not a matter of brown, yellow or white. I would contend that it is often a red herring. I would like to imagine myself as being a child of Singapore. Both my parents were born and bred here. My father's ancestors were from Kerala in India, my mother's from Holland. So what does that make me? Indian? Eurasian? Or just plain confused? My birth certificate adopts the race of my father. But by the time I was old enough to have an identity card of my own, a less male-oriented regime held sway at the registry, and I was labelled a Eurasian. And what, I wonder, will be the racial tag attached to the issue of my sister, soon to be married to an Englishman? Anglo-Indian? Euro-Eurasian? Other-others?

Such racial semantics have never bothered me unduly, for I know who I am, whatever the bureaucrats choose to call me. But it would do away with much confusion and spare administrators considerable anguish if we could simply be left to be what we really are. That is, Singaporean. After all, one is not made any less of an Indian, Malay or Chinese for not having to endlessly remind oneself of the fact by writing it down on forms and documents. The real issue then is how we get our people to shift from being just Chinese, Indians or Malays, who happen to be citizens of Singapore, to being Chinese, Malay or Indian Singaporeans. The difference is ostensibly small, but its meaning is not slight.

This will be the test of nationhood. Pass that one, and we might well be on our way to becoming a 'great little nation'.

(First published 26 August 1990)

141

Race is not the only divide among Singaporeans. Indeed, the language divide between English-educated Chinese Singaporeans and their Chinese-educated counterparts has been as deep and politically problematic as any other, if not more so.

Are Singaporeans on different political wavelengths?

IS THE electorate here politically split on linguistic lines? This question was raised recently by Brigadier-General (NS) George Yeo. His thesis was as simple as it was intriguing: Broadly speaking, there are two groups of voters here – the Channel 5 and the Channel 8 voters. Channel 8 voters refer to the Chinese-educated Singaporeans who are likely to go on voting for the ruling People's Action Party so long as it delivers material prosperity, and Channel 5 voters are the English-educated Singaporeans who clamour for more political liberalisation.

A prudent government, suggested BG Yeo, would always ensure that it met the material aspirations of the Channel 8 voters, who formed the majority. This conservative force would thus slow down the pace of political reform.

But if this led to frustrated Channel 5 Singaporeans voting with their feet, the nation's economic prospects would be dampened, thereby undermining the government's support among Channel 8 voters. As I see it, the message to those at the talk, mainly Channel 5 voters, was this – ultimately, liberalisation would come, but the pace of change would have to be moderated so that the majority could be carried along by the winds of change.

An interesting view indeed. But would Channel 5 voters subscribe to it? No. At least not yet. For two reasons.

First, because the dichotomy between Channel 5 and 8 voters is too much of a simplification to be a useful electoral rule of thumb (and it is no more than that). More channels are needed to properly reflect Singapore's disparate electorate.

Second, and more important, because these various groups have yet to tune in to each other. Perhaps a four-channel system would better reflect the Republic's electoral dynamics. In this fourfold categorisation, Channel 8 voters would refer to the roughly 600,000 Chinese-educated Singaporeans, who form what BG Yeo termed the government's 'HDB heartlands'. Channel 5 voters would be the group of nearly 750,000 English-educated Singaporeans, who may like the idea of a scaled-down government, but not at the price of scaled-down bonuses.

Then there is the Channel 12 (the precursor of today's Arts Central) group of about 140,000 English-educated professionals, who are highly vocal in their demands for a more liberal political climate here. A last group would be the Channel 10 voters, comprising some 60,000 or so Chinese-educated intellectuals, who, while passionate in their defence of things Chinese, probably share more in common with their Chinese-educated compatriots than their English-educated counterparts. The divisions among the electorate are thus not along just linguistic lines. Age, educational background, profession and class are also significant.

How does this four-channel division apply? Consider some issues. On the question of how the Chinese language or culture might be promoted or the recent proposal to have multilingual signs here to give the city more of an Asian 'feel', the split is more clearly along linguistic and not racial or other lines.

But take the issue of dual citizenship: While Channel 12 voters urge Singaporeans not only to have a more global outlook but also to show more 'generosity of spirit' towards emigrants who wish to return home, I suspect that the majority here – the Channel 5 and 8 voters – are affronted by the thought that those who have 'spurned the nation' should be wooed back.

On R-rated films: Whereas Channel 12 liberals take it as a virtual article of faith that less censorship would be universally desired, it is becoming increasingly clear that many Channel 5 and 8 voters disagree. For example, during one of his community visits, some parents urged Goh Chok Tong not to relax censorship rules, for fear that it would undermine Singapore's Asian values. Mr Goh replied, 'Please speak up. Make your views known. If you remain silent, when the others clamour for us to liberalise, we will have to relax the rules.'

Now this is interesting. By encouraging more open discussion of these issues, Mr Goh is helping the voters from the various channels to tune in to one another. If handled well, this process could make Singaporeans more aware that there are times when each group's aspirations will have to be reconciled with other competing interests in society.

The danger remains, however, that taken to extremes, open debate could fill the airwaves here with static and fuzz. Furthermore, while more discussion may help Singaporeans appreciate the views on other channels, this does not mean that before long, everyone here is likely to be followers of the same political programmes. A plural society will always have groups that see issues from different perspectives. But so long as there is a broad consensus among all Singaporeans on the major issues, it will not matter unduly that they tune in to different channels. Trying to create a one-view, one-channel Singapore is likely to lead to less pleasant viewing all round.

(First published 25 July 1991)

Language policy and the mother tongue are hot issues that every government leader in Singapore has had to handle with care, even if his party has an overwhelming majority in Parliament. Having to carry the Chinese ground at every election to keep their hold on power has meant that PAP leaders have had to perform a careful balancing act, always bearing in mind the concerns of this group, even as they strove to act in the national interest.

Singapore still walks language tightrope

IN POLITICALLY quiet Singapore, not a few foreign observers and even some Singaporeans are wont to say that politics is dead. After all, there seems scarcely any dramatic partisan politicking, factional infighting or public demonstrations to behold. The government, it would seem, goes about doing what it must, and the people get on with their lives, labour and loves.

Anyone who subscribes to this view of how this country is governed should have sat through the four-hour debate on the new Chinese language policy in Parliament on Wednesday. On display were the competing societal forces that exist below the surface, and which well up from time to time when any issue impinging on race, language or religion arises.

First, there were the English-educated MPs, welcoming the move that would ease the language burden on English-speaking families. Most memorable was Hong Kah GRC MP Kenneth Chen who recounted the 'bitterness' his son still harbours at being denied a place in a junior college because he could not pass Chinese, even while he breezed through his other subjects.

Set against this group of English-educated Chinese were those from the other side of the old language divide. (No doubt the chasm between the Chinese- and English-educated has narrowed considerably in recent years, as seen from the eloquent calls by English-educated MPs to young Singaporeans to pay heed to their mother-tongue classes. But it is arguably still the deepest schism in Singapore's body politic.) Led most consistently by MPs Peh Chin Hua and Ow Chin Hock, this group welcomed the new policy, especially the move to allow more students to do Higher Chinese. But there was no mistaking the way their speeches were laced with concerns that language standards might fall, while the numbers of students choosing the 'soft option' Chinese-language course might rise over time. They wanted safeguards and caps to prevent this, more incentives to promote the learning of Chinese, more Chinese-language schools and even a Chinese university.

Add to this heady mix, the opposition, with Workers' Party member Low Thia Khiang making some telling interventions on the implications of the new policy, and Singapore People's Party chief Chiam See Tong taking up, surprisingly, the call for a Chinese university here.

Not to be left out, too, were the minority MPs and the fervent multiculturalists, whose standard bearer these days seems to be Senior Parliamentary Secretary for Foreign Affairs Zainul Abidin Rasheed. They wanted assurances that the new language policy will be applied to Malay and Tamil as well. Make no bones about it, but every proposal to raise the status of the Chinese language, promote its learning, or to nurture a 'Chinese elite' touches a raw nerve in the minorities, anxious that the multiracial flavour of this country and its commitment to fair treatment for all races should never be eroded.

Amid all these contesting voices, ministers had to tread a fine line. They were quick to make clear that if there was a need for a Malay or Tamil basic course, there will be one. They added that the Chinese language review was meant to address a real problem faced by Chinese families here, and in no way overturned the commitment to English as the common working language.

The policy package that Lee Hsien Loong unveiled was also balanced carefully to help carry the ground on various fronts. The move to introduce a simpler Chinese syllabus for the minority struggling with the language, and to revise textbooks to make them less difficult, was set against plans to boost the numbers taking Higher Chinese as part of the effort to train a new generation of Chinese educators, journalists, broadcasters, MPs and ministers, a group that has been loosely – and unfortunately – called the 'Chinese elite'. (It is an unhelpful term as it raises needless hackles. Try, perhaps, the term 'Chinese community leaders' instead.)

When the debate had all but been wrapped up in English, it was telling that Mr Lee saw a need to switch channels as it were, to summarise the discussion in his mother tongue. Speaking in fluent Mandarin that would have left many wondering how he had scored only a grade 4 for Chinese in school, he addressed the Chinese ground directly, in an effort to win their support and understanding for the new move.

Whether or not this package wins acceptance now remains to be seen. Certainly, there is still much explaining and convincing to be done, especially among the Chinese-educated, sensitive about the erosion of standards and the concessions to their English-speaking counterparts.

Indeed, some conundrums remain: If the move to introduce CL 'B' is necessary because the proportion of English-speaking families has doubled from 20 per cent to 40 per cent of the Primary 1 cohort between 1988 and 1998, what happens when this rises again to 60 per cent or higher some years down the road?

And in the midst of the pervasive influence of the Western media and its values, is there not a need to do more to inculcate traditional values in the young, adopting innovative media-age methods to do so?

These are difficult questions, all the more so since whatever ideal solutions educationists conjure up have to be set against the realities of what students can cope with, and the emotional, social and academic price they pay to do so. An uphill struggle with Chinese risks turning some against their mother tongue and culture, or worse, causing them to uproot entirely to other shores where their talents are less hampered by language demands, an increasingly real problem in a globally connected world.

So, willy-nilly, language policy will have to be based on practical realities, both in terms of what students can achieve and what is achievable politically. This is how it has always been and how it is likely to remain for a long time to come.

In his memoirs, for example, Senior Minister Lee Kuan Yew recounts how a government committee in the 1950s grappled with the very same issue – the rising number of English-educated households and the need to change language policy, which would no doubt provoke a clash with the then highly volatile Chinese ground. Years later, in the 1960s, similar issues had to be confronted. As Mr Lee noted in *Lee Kuan Yew: The Man and His Ideas*, 'The big decision was made in

1965 ... we decided to do it by evolution, not by suddenly deciding, "Right, English is the working language, and we'll also learn our mother tongues." I think there would have been riots. The Chinese would never have accepted that. So we said, "We leave things as they are. Don't change it. But parents can decide..." By that policy, we knew that over time it would lead to English as the working language. Indeed, it turned out that way.'

Evolution continues. Echoes of this were heard in the reply in Parliament by Education Minister Teo Chee Hean to those calling for more Chinese schools here. He was quick to point out that since 1991, there has been not a single candidate for the ME3 course, which allows students to learn more Mandarin and less English.

The upshot of Wednesday's debate was this: even in 1999, the politics of language in this heterogeneous society is alive indeed. Visitors and even some Singaporeans who remark on the ease with which the various races here get along with each other often fail to see the delicate balancing act that is needed to keep these visceral issues on an even keel, not just by ministers and MPs, but by a whole array of community leaders, educationists, those in the media and citizens.

These days, few people doubt that the different ethnic strands in the Singaporean thread give it strength. But no one should imagine that it cannot also fray all too easily. A quick look through the headlines in recent times shows churches being burnt down, women being raped and rampaging mobs attacking Muslim clerics, not so far from our shores. They should be all the reminder anyone needs.

(First published 23 January 1999)

As a relatively young society, Singapore has come round rather late to the idea of the need to pass on its collective memories and values to the young. It has started a National Education programme, which has sparked some controversy. Yet, efforts by communities to preserve age-old values and wisdoms are as old as the hills, with some having mastered the means to do so better than others.

Tell them a story

A STORY I have been told since boyhood, of the bloodshed in Singapore's streets during the race riots of 1964, remains with me to this day. My father was holed up at the office. Riots had broken out in the streets not far from our house in Joo Chiat Place. The telephone lines were down. He had no way of reaching my mother, alone at home, to tell her what had happened, or to find out how she was. Oblivious to the fracas outside, my mother ventured to the shops with my newborn sister, only to stumble onto the mayhem in the streets. Thankfully, my father managed somehow to rush home, found my mother and retreated indoors, away from the madding crowd.

This story is repeated often, with varying degrees of embellishment, at family gatherings. It resurfaced recently due to the discussion about Singapore's history. For me, the tale resonates every time I hear accounts of ethnic violence, here and abroad. Among these is the infamous Maria Hertogh case in 1950, when Christians and Muslims here, forgetting all godly injunctions against killing their neighbours, went about their ungodly business of religious revenge.

Budding journalists here are told how an editor's decision to use a picture of the girl, clad in Muslim dress, kneeling before a Christian statue, caused passions to run over, spilling blood in the streets. The message of these stories for me is simple, yet powerful: Never take racial peace for granted. Respect all religions. Try to get along.

So even as educationists ponder how to implement Goh Chok Tong's call last week to devise a new National Education curriculum to bring Singapore's history, vulnerabilities and constraints home to today's young, the answer seems clear to me: Tell them a story. Yes, a story. One that is short and simple, but which they are unlikely to forget.

Now, this idea, I confess, is not new. It is, in fact, as old as time, having been used by the early Christian chroniclers. Those Christians knew what they were doing. Eager to spread the word about their new religious leader, they chose not to expound the intricacies of Christian doctrine. Instead, they told a compelling story of a boy born in a manger one winter's night in Bethlehem, who grew up to be persecuted for what he preached, and was crucified on a cross. Whether you believe it or not, it is not a story you soon forget.

Other communities took up the idea. Every Frenchman knows how Joan of Arc was burned at the stake. There is even a public square and Cathedral in Rouen to mark that gory event. Every time the story is told it celebrates French courage and evokes national pride. Similarly, the Americans have tales about the Pilgrim Fathers, and George Washington taking his hatchet to his cherry tree.

What about Singapore? We too need stories to capture the defining moments from our collective past, as well as the features that make us a distinctive society. One that I have heard recounts how Senior Minister Lee Kuan Yew's anticolonial sentiments were first aroused. It was a good, tight slap on the face by a Japanese soldier that did it.

The impact of the blow set off a train of thoughts: Why should he be treated in this way? And where were his British protectors? Similar notions in the minds of others led to the rise of the anticolonial resistance movement.

Tell them that story. Tell them also how the same firebrand Lee fought back tears when announcing Singapore's expulsion from the Malaysian federation, the enormity of the event hitting him even as he broke the news to his countrymen.

Tell them stories not just about leading figures, but also about everyday things and events that have featured in Singaporeans' collective experience. So just as the potato carries special meaning for Irishmen, after the potato famine in the 19th century caused many to starve and drove hordes to leave for the New World, Singaporean hearts should stir at the sight of the humble tapioca, on which many were kept alive during the Japanese Occupation.

Tell them these stories not just in words, but in images too. A picture I once came across remains etched in my mind. It was of Singapore's first Cabinet, standing in their all-white outfits. The future must have seemed daunting. But you would not have spotted it in the determination on the faces of the young Lee Kuan Yew, Goh Keng Swee, Toh Chin Chye and S. Rajaratnam. Those figures cast in stone and set at the very scene – on the steps of City Hall – would be a striking testimony to the men who set this country on its present course.

Tell the young these stories, not just in words and images, but also in deeds. The ancient Chinese gave us dragon boat races and dumpling festivals to commemorate a poignant event: how fishermen threw rice into the rivers to prevent fish feeding on the body of patriot Qu Yuan, who drowned himself in despair at the misery around him. The quirky British mark Guy Fawkes Day. They celebrate his failed attempt to blow up their Parliament building, by ironically lighting up the London sky with a burst of fireworks. The reason: Had Fawkes succeeded, there would have been fireworks indeed, albeit of a rather different kind.

In Singapore, such historical celebrations are few and far between. Take Community Day, for example, which was held on July 21 with much fun and games. No mention was made of the race riots cited above, which occurred on that very day 32 years ago, leaving at least 460 people injured and 23 dead. Could it be that no one remembered? Or was it thought unwise to rake up unpleasant memories? Maybe someone feared that highlighting those unhappy events might upset our neighbours? Yet, unless one remembers the past, how will a younger generation learn from the follies of earlier ones? Choosing to ignore past pain leaves present joys less deeply felt. It is also the surest way to return to unhappy times.

My suggestion: Let future Community Days not be glib celebrations of racial tolerance, but also telling reminders of the times when things were not so rosy. Yes, tell them the story.

These tales, legends and myths are the stuff that binds a people together. Happy or sad, simple yet profound, they can help unite disparate groups into a nation. Bringing history to the young will require more than just rewriting the history syllabus for schools here. Singaporeans, old and young, will have to remember and relive their shared past. Then, hopefully one day, the young will come to feel that these stories are their story too.

(First published 14 September 1996)

Stop that crooked bridge

At the height of the controversy surrounding bilateral ties, would Malaysia have agreed to a demand from Singapore to stop building its 'crooked bridge' in Johor – immediately? Driving on such a steep and winding bridge might be unsafe. A joint panel should study this. The strange bridge might leave a negative impression on foreign visitors who will surely wonder how and why such a structure was built. Could the two countries not agree? Was someone tipsy, or on the take, when the project was approved? Perhaps an international poll should be done on this? In the meantime, all work on the bridge should be halted, at once, for as long as it takes, to address these concerns.

This idea, of course, is laughable, almost as funny as the design of the proposed bridge.

(From 'Will second causeway be a bridge too far?'
26 April 1997, see page 170)

Chapter 6
Malaysia-Singapore ties:
Will squabbles never cease?

THE PICTURES were as refreshing as they were familiar. The prime ministers of Singapore and Malaysia, smiling, shaking hands as they savoured the new rapprochement between their two countries. The media hailed it as a sign that Malaysia's new Prime Minister Abdullah Badawi was heralding a new age, after the rancorous Mahathir years, and offering new ideas on how to resolve the conundrums in bilateral ties.

The sunnier prospects for bilateral ties came as a relief. But having seen, up close, similar scenes of newfound bilateral bonhomie, I could not help but remain a little sceptical. I recalled a similar news event not so long ago, when Goh Chok Tong and Dr Mahathir Mohamad met one sunny morning at the opening of the second link between Singapore and Johor. There were happy faces and optimistic speeches all round about what the future might hold. I wrote the news reports and analysis pieces that day about a 'turning point' in ties. Alas, the tide soon turned again, as relations were plunged into a frosty storm of disputes just months later. The pattern would be repeated throughout the 1990s, giving rise to fatigue among journalists – and the public at large, I suspect – at the seemingly endless bilateral spats. Whether they are over water, railway land, air space, toll charges or land reclamation, the way in which issues cropped up every now and again and never seemed to get resolved has soured relations.

Take, for example, the latest dispute over Singapore's land reclamation projects. By most accounts, Singapore won Round One of the fight over its reclamation works in Tuas and Pulau Tekong. Malaysia had pushed to get the work halted immediately by asking the International Tribunal for the Law of the Sea (Itlos) to issue a 'stop work' order against Singapore, only to be rebuffed by the judges in Hamburg.

The gritty saga did not end there. The second stage entailed a separate arbitration panel to study the Malaysian claims that the reclamation is causing permanent damage to its environment and encroaching on its territory. Singapore says it is confident that this is not the case, and has studies to back this up. The legal battle will continue for many more months. But long after the dust has settled, the unpleasant memory of the unfortunate way in which Malaysia chose to settle this dispute will remain.

Malaysia had raised a hue and cry about Singapore's reclamation work since January 2002. But despite repeated requests from Singapore to back up its case, it failed to do so until 4 July 2003. Then, out of the blue, it gave Singapore two weeks to stop its reclamation works or face a summons to the international court. In other words, it took Malaysia 18 months to make its case on why it was concerned about the reclamation. But it gave Singapore just 14 days to respond and comply.

How is that for being 'insensitive' to a neighbour, a charge often hurled at Singapore?

What followed was a round of bilateral talks on the issue in August 2003. Even as plans were being made for further discussions, Malaysia unilaterally called these off on September 5 and took matters to the tribunal in Hamburg. And after the case was brought before the court, Malaysian leaders and editors continued to press their line: Singapore should stop work immediately. Not to do so was to be 'stubborn' and 'insensitive', they railed.

The normally sensible Umno Youth chief Hishammuddin Hussein (now Education Minister) joined in, charging that Singapore was committing a 'contemptuous act' against the international court by failing to halt its reclamation works. 'What we are concerned about now is Singapore's method in handling relations with our country which may provoke anger among our people,' he declared.

Well put. Funny thing is, the argument applies both ways.

Indeed, soon after the ruling in favour of Singapore was announced in Hamburg, Malaysia's then Prime Minister Mahathir Mohamad seemed to brush the verdict aside. He declared, 'What we want is for them to stop work now, that's all, and we will go for final arbitration.'

In other words, never mind what the world's judges said (reclamation should be allowed to continue as there is no pressing reason to stop it right away), never mind what the technical experts said (there is no evidence of serious impact on the environment), Singapore should just stop work, now, because Malaysia says so.

Malaysian leaders must know that no Singapore government worth its salt would, or could, agree to that, without causing anger and bewilderment among its people. To do so would be tantamount to giving up an independent country's right to decide when and where it might undertake projects within its own territory, even after the most rigorous of tests to ensure that these have no impact on any neighbours' interests.

Just consider the reverse situation: At the height of the controversy surrounding bilateral ties, would Malaysia have agreed to a demand from Singapore to stop building its 'crooked bridge' in Johor – immediately? Driving on such a steep and winding bridge might be unsafe. A joint panel should study this. The strange bridge might leave a negative impression on foreign visitors who will surely wonder how and why such a structure was built. Could the two countries not agree? Was someone tipsy, or on the take, when the project was approved? Perhaps an international poll should be done on this? In the meantime, all work on the bridge should be halted, at once, for as long as it takes to address these concerns.

This idea, of course, is laughable, almost as funny as the design of the proposed bridge.

Indeed, Malaysians, I suspect, know that their case against Singapore's reclamation is on shaky ground. That explains why its media felt a need to shield its readers from the implications of the outcome of the legal adventure in Hamburg. Consider the following headlines, which reflect how the court's verdict was viewed around the world:

❖ *Asian Wall Street Journal*: Singapore wins round in dispute with Malaysia
❖ Reuters: UN Court rejects Malaysian plea on land reclamation
❖ Dow Jones International News: Singapore can continue Straits Reclamation
❖ *The Straits Times*: Round one to Singapore
❖ Bernama news agency (Malaysia): Itlos decision a great success for Malaysia, says Syed Hamid
❖ *The New Straits Times* (Malaysia): Tribunal decision: Singapore must not cause irreparable prejudice to Malaysia's rights
❖ *The Star* (Malaysia): Save The Straits, Tribunal directs Singapore not to harm environs with reclamation work.

Is it not curious how the world's media came to one conclusion about what the Hamburg judges had ruled while Malaysian editors came to quite another? Perhaps it was just a case of poor news judgement. But by focusing on other aspects of the judges' statements, such as the call for an independent panel to monitor the reclamation – which Singapore had offered even before the court case – the Malaysian media managed to shield their readers from the fact that the court had dismissed Malaysia's main point: its insistence that work had to be stopped immediately.

The following day, it was the same old story: Singapore's *Straits Times* read: KL must accept decision – Abdullah; Malaysia's *New Straits Times* said: DPM – Set up panel quickly.

To be fair, Datuk Seri Abdullah did say that he accepted the Itlos decision although he was not entirely happy with it. This was mentioned in some Malaysian reports, which led off, however, with the then DPM's call for an international panel to oversee the reclamation to be set up quickly. Some reports also repeated allegations, which Singapore has refuted, that the reclamation work was being speeded up quietly and renewed the calls for it to be halted.

Pardon me, but might not the Malaysian reaction to the court's verdict be characterised as a 'contemptuous act' against Itlos, to borrow Datuk Hishammuddin's pungent phrase? Might Singapore, too, not wonder about Malaysia's 'method in handling relations with our country which might provoke anger among our people'?

Indeed, the reclamation dispute is just one of several in which the two sides have decided to resort to arbitration, instead of trying to settle the matter amicably between the two countries through give-and-take. The dispute over Pedra Branca has been referred to the International Court of Justice in The Hague. There has been much talk about settling the longstanding water issue through arbitration. Perhaps even the differences over the Points of Agreement covering Malaysia's customs operations and railway land in Singapore might need to be settled in this way.

Will the squabbles never cease? First, the two countries disagree on an issue. Then, they quarrel over how to settle it. Even when a neutral party adjudicates, the cavilling continues on how to interpret the verdict.

Lamentably, what becomes clear from these developments is that however the present legal saga plays out, this sorry cycle of bilateral spats might well continue. It gives credence to the view that perhaps the inherent differences in the way the two societies are structured will put them at odds for a long time to come. That leaves a bitter taste in the mouth of many Singaporeans. So much so that Singaporeans were prepared to drink recycled or desalinated water if this was necessary to overcome the country's water shortage, since progress on the water talks with Malaysia seemed all but hopeless. Ironically, the Singapore government was helped in its efforts to promote the use of Newater by Malaysian officials, albeit unwittingly.

Must it be that way? Are bilateral ties doomed to being fraught forever? Malaysia's Prime Minister Abdullah Badawi has offered some hope of a way forward. Since taking over the premiership, he has brought a wave of fresh air and thinking to bilateral ties, showing signs that perhaps good sense might yet prevail in ending the seemingly endless bickering. He has asked that the proposals for the 'crooked bridge' be relooked. He has suggested that new ideas might be put on the table, starting with moves to tackle some of the 'low hanging' fruit, resolving those issues which are easier to set aside, even if more complex ones will take more time and effort to settle. Singapore has welcomed these overtures cautiously, but made plain that should these lead nowhere, it would prefer that issues which can't be settled be sent to a third party for adjudication, so that they do not continue to dog relations. Yet, one wonders if even this would put an end to the tiresome and wasteful squabbles of recent years.

Who wins and who loses from this endless cycle of bilateral spats? No one. The real losers are the people of both Malaysia and Singapore, who see more and more opportunities for their countries to work together being wasted, like sand slipping away in an hourglass.

The ups and downs in Malaysia-Singapore ties went through an especially bad patch in 1997, when Malaysia threatened to freeze ties in the wake of comments by Singapore leaders, which annoyed them. But as is always the case in this bilateral relationship, there was more to it than met the eye.

Playing *wayang kulit* with KL-Singapore ties?

AS YOU read this, dozens of Singaporeans are making their way across the Causeway to Johor. Barring any unexpected delays of the sort experienced last weekend, when customs officials seemed to be on an unofficial 'go-slow', more than 25,000 visitors, both Singaporean as well as foreign tourists, would have entered Malaysia by the end of the day. Many will head for one of Johor's 27 golf courses or its fine beaches for a weekend away. Others will go to one of the state's spanking new malls and supermarkets, to shop for everything from food to clothes and video CDs. In all, these visitors will spend an estimated M$2 million (S$1.14 million) to M$3 million, according to Johor's state tourism chairman Jimmy Low, quoted in the *Far Eastern Economic Review*.

Singapore firms are also the largest investors in Johor, securing M$3.2 billion in investment licences in the state last year. The Republic was the largest foreign investor in Malaysia, pumping in M$5 billion last year, ahead of Japan and the United States, and accounting for nearly 30 per cent of all overseas investments. Malaysia is also one of Singapore's largest trading partners. According to a Malaysian Finance Ministry report, trade with Singapore rose 9 per cent to

M\$37.6 billion in the first seven months of last year. These economic figures reflect the ties of geography, culture and history between the two countries, symbolised by the 1.2 kilometre Causeway that links them.

A second land-link is scheduled to be opened in October, and there is already talk that Johor is interested in having a third causeway with Singapore. Little wonder then that Goh Chok Tong described relations between the two countries as being 'like water, which cannot be cut even by a knife', as the Malay saying goes. Or as Malaysian Investors' Association president H.S. Lim puts it, 'The commercial ties remain strong ... the furore will fade away.'

NOT so fast, say Malaysian leaders, insisting that 'it will take time' for relations to return to their previous level, following the recent row over Senior Minister Lee Kuan Yew's statement about Johor being 'notorious for shootings, muggings and car-jackings'. Then came the stunning reports quoting unnamed Malaysian Cabinet ministers saying that all fresh bilateral ties would be frozen, including government-to-government contacts and the granting of contracts to Singapore firms.

The day after, it seemed that it was all a figment of the media's fertile imagination, with ministers 'clarifying' that the reports were 'not quite accurate' and that there had been no decision to freeze ties after all. Sighs of relief were heaved all round at this more positive gloss put on that fateful Cabinet meeting. Questions were raised: Was Malaysian Prime Minister Dr Mahathir Mohamad privy to the decision? Which ministers leaked the information, and why? And what did Deputy Prime Minister Anwar Ibrahim, who chaired the meeting, have to say about the odd turn of events? Why were ministers still insisting that some ties, such as sports and cultural links, would be 'suspended'?

But such idle speculation was put aside. The Malaysian Cabinet chose to dwell on other more pressing matters of state at its latest meeting last Wednesday. Nor, apparently, did it discuss Mr Goh's response to these developments as well as his proposal of several 'worthwhile projects' both sides could work together on to boost ties.

If the unspoken message from these developments was unclear, it was hammered home this week. On Thursday, Malaysian Culture, Arts and Tourism Minister Datuk Sabbaruddin Chik chose not to attend the Destination Malaysia tourism fair he was scheduled to open here, saying he was too busy. Ironically, he sent his officials to declare 'business as usual' and proclaim Malaysia's desire to draw more visitors from here. Earlier in the week, Works Minister Datuk Seri S. Samy Vellu, surveying with satisfaction the progress on the second causeway between the two countries, said that there was a 'possibility' that the bridge opening ceremony might be attended by Dr Mahathir. Only weeks ago, Johor Mentri Besar Datuk Abdul Ghani Othman had said that the bridge would be opened officially in October by the prime ministers of both countries.

So the question arises whether Malaysia and Singapore ties are now to fall into a *wayang kulit* phase, with diplomatic games being played out as both sides edge coyly, tentatively, towards a new, perhaps not so warm, embrace. That would be a pity. Mr Goh, trying hard to remain ever gracious and friendly, has said repeatedly that Singapore stands ready to do its part to improve ties, but would do so at a pace that Malaysia is comfortable with. He also, perhaps wisely, chose not to be drawn when asked by reporters about Malaysian leaders' comments about difficulties they faced in 'being friends with Singapore'. In particular, they chose to make public their unhappiness over the two issues of Malayan Railway land and the Royal Malaysian Naval Base in Woodlands. Such delicate matters, said Mr Goh, were best not discussed through media reports and could be settled more amicably in private. Significantly, too, newspaper reports of a decision by the Malaysian Cabinet to go ahead with plans to build a bridge to replace the present Causeway appeared even before the Singapore government was approached officially on the idea. Mr Goh has said he 'would certainly look into' the bridge proposal and appeared to welcome the idea, if such a plan was communicated to the Singapore side officially. This seems sensible. After all, have not media reports proven to be 'not quite accurate' before?

THE MOST worrying thing about this unhappy saga is the nagging doubt that there is more to it all than meets the eye. Let me be clear: Singaporeans understand that Malaysians were upset by SM Lee's remarks. Rightly, Mr Lee apologised, quickly and unreservedly, even agreeing to have the offending words removed from his affidavit to the courts. But the vitriol that has been heaped on Singapore by some Malaysian politicians and groups, coupled with the reluctance in the response to efforts to make up and move on, cannot but cause some to wonder if there is more on Malaysian minds.

Indeed, even the authoritative *London Financial Times* has questioned if the motive behind the Kuala Lumpur government's statement that it was freezing bilateral ties with Singapore was not aimed at prising concessions on projects Malaysia was pushing. The editorial headlined 'Rough Straits' argued that, if this were the case, there would be a high price to be paid. 'It is not only the grave risks inherent in open confrontation with neighbours. Malaysia itself will be divided if its sizeable Chinese minority is alienated as a result. Asean values call for calm and consensus. It's time they were applied.'

It added: 'Care is called for on both sides: sparks can cause blazes. The flames would not need much fanning to undermine stability in a region which is one of the high points of Asia's economic success.'

A case of the Western media reading too much into Asian ways it does not understand? Perhaps. Let us hope so.

Water, they say, cannot be cut with a knife. Singaporeans and Malaysians, enjoying the mutual benefits of cooperation, certainly want this to continue. But the waters can be calmed only if knives are put aside and not used to whip up political waves needlessly.

(First published 5 April 1997)

169

In 1997, from out of the blue, some Malaysian leaders called for new levies on Singaporeans heading to Malaysia to ease congestion there, just as the second link to Malaysia was to be opened. In the spirit of good relations, I proposed some countermeasures, with tongue firmly in cheek.

Will second causeway be a bridge too far?

A TRIP to Malaysia could cost you between M$20 and M$50 more if the Johor state government goes ahead with a proposal to slap a levy on Singapore visitors to the state. The reason: Johor's streets are clogged up because too many Singaporean shoppers drive their cars into the state. Welcoming the levy idea, Malaysian Transport Minister Datuk Seri Ling Liong Sik said on Wednesday that it was worth considering if it helped the state solve its traffic jams, which had 'tremendous economic costs'. 'You waste time, miss appointments, and activities do not run smoothly. We only get frustrated by all these,' he said.

Ever so quickly, others jumped on the levy bandwagon. The Federation of Malaysian Consumers Association (Fomca) has called on the Malaysian government to slap a M$50 levy on Singapore-registered cars entering Johor. Fomca blames Singaporeans for the high cost of living in Johor and believes that restricting the number of Singaporean visitors to the state would help keep costs in check. Joining in, the Johor Tourist Association also backed the levy idea, saying it would help reduce traffic congestion in Johor. JTA chairman Tengku Jamailah Tengku Archibald, however, went on to add that he did not think the levy would lead to fewer tourists from Singapore going to Johor. 'Malaysia, and Johor in particular, have so much to offer Singaporean visitors. I doubt they will stop coming just because of the levy,' he said.

But this argument is odd. If the levy will not reduce the number of Singaporean visitors, and so not cut down the traffic congestion – the very *raison d'être* for the levy – why have the levy at all?

MOST Singaporeans, I believe, do not wish to be a nuisance to their neighbours. They travel to Johor because they are drawn by the good and inexpensive food, the open spaces, entertainment spots and, for the most part, the friendliness of the Malaysian people. But some Malaysian leaders appear unhappy about the number of Singaporean visitors to their country and would rather have fewer of them about. That is a pity.

But, in the spirit of good neighborliness, here are some suggestions, off the top of my head, on how to discourage the 20,000 Singaporeans who cross the Causeway every day from doing so.

❖ Full-tank rule. Singapore might as well go the whole hog and raise the present three-quarter tank rule (requiring cars to have at least three-quarters of their petrol tank full before going across the Causeway) to a full tank. Finance Minister Richard Hu has said repeatedly that the aim of the rule is not to discourage Singaporeans from going to Johor, but to keep the revenue lost from duties on petrol bought outside the Republic to about $1 million a month. Having a full-tank rule would mean no loss in petrol duties at all. This revenue could be put to an endless number of good uses, from giving scholarships to university students, from here or other Asean countries, to helping the less well-off cope with the round of higher transport fares announced this week. Sure, some Singaporeans would end up paying a little more for that additional quarter tank of petrol. But their higher spending would translate into more earnings for oil companies here, which could then employ more attendants at their kiosks. More money, more jobs, more spending, all of which would rev the economic engines here.

❖ A levy of our own. Rather than burdening Malaysian officials with having to collect the proposed levy, why not do it for them by collecting it at the Singapore end of the Causeway? The result, presumably, would be the same: less congestion in Johor. But having more Singaporeans staying at home, and perhaps even shopping here, might bring customers back to the many malls here. The millions that Singaporean visitors are said to spend in Johor's spanking new shopping centres would certainly go a long way to bringing relief to the Republic's retail sector. The estimated M$200,000 to $500,000 a day that might be earned from the levy would also come in handy. One suggestion: use it to pay for youth exchanges between Umno Youth and other youth groups here to promote better understanding.

❖ Higher levy on Malaysian cars: While we are at it, it might be noted that, like the good Datuk Ling, Singaporeans also get frustrated by traffic jams, missed appointments and activities not going on as planned. Perhaps having fewer Malaysian cars on Singapore's streets, especially Orchard Road on weekends, might help. Malaysian-registered cars are now given 68 days' free entry here, which includes 52 Sundays, 11 public holidays and five other days. They pay S$20 for every additional day here. Might not a simple flat S$20 levy per entry be, shall we say, more efficient?

NOW, I must add that these are just suggestions thought out loud, which must be studied carefully before proceeding with them. After all, to borrow the words of Johor's Datuk Ghani, 'this issue will have to be discussed in detail because decisions made would implicate both Malaysia and Singapore'. I have a suspicion, though, that detailed studies might find them unwise and perhaps even unnecessary, since the free and easy access that citizens on both sides of the Causeway now enjoy is mutually beneficial.

WHAT is most curious, however, is the timing of this new move to curb the number of Singapore visitors to Malaysia. Do not get me wrong. Malaysia has every right to do so, if it feels that it is in its best interests. But coming in the wake of the recent diplomatic row between the two countries as it does, the proposal cannot but raise questions about the motives behind it.

Ironically, too, the plan to keep the number of Singaporean visitors to Johor down appears set to coincide with the imminent opening of the second causeway linking Singapore to Johor. Perhaps I am wrong, but I would imagine that the causeway was built to enable more, not fewer, visits between the countries. Indeed, when up and running, 200,000 vehicles will be able to cross the 2 km long bridge every day. These will carry tourists, shoppers, investors and relatives from Singapore to Johor and beyond, adding to the boom in the economy there, but also, inevitably, to the congestion. Yet, despite their concerns about a deluge of Singaporeans, Johor is said to have proposed building a third causeway. The upshot of this is plain: when the plan for the M$1.6 billion second link was unveiled, it was hailed by Malaysians and Singaporeans alike as being yet another solid symbol of the close ties between the two countries.

The opening of the second link therefore offers an ideal opportunity for leaders from both countries to signal their willingness and intention to take Malaysia and Singapore to new levels in ties and cooperation among their peoples. It will be lamentable indeed if, instead of seizing this opportunity, politicians turn the other way. That would make the second causeway a sure testimony, not to the ties that bind, but to the deep breach that still needs to be bridged.

(First published 26 April 1997)

Stringent customs checks, rainstorms and missing staff were among the mystifying reasons cited for the sudden emergence of a long tailback of lorries at the Causeway in October 1997. It clogged up the vital economic link between the two countries, prompting me to suggest some ways to get the traffic flowing again.

How to put an end to the sorry lorry saga

YOU might call it a sorry lorry saga. Nearly a month ago, officials from Johor's Customs and Excise Department began checks on all lorries crossing the Causeway, ostensibly to deter tax evasion and smuggling. Then came word that the stringent checks were needed because some firms were rushing to import more goods into Malaysia in an attempt to beat rumoured increases in import duties. Delays were later said to have occurred because Customs officials had to close shop to await the announcement of the Malaysian Budget to see if import levies were indeed changed. Later, when new and higher levies were imposed on an array of goods, these officials fumbled with the unfamiliar paperwork, causing more holdups.

But the prize for the most inventive explanation for the jams must surely go to the Johor Chinese Chamber of Commerce (JCCC). It issued a statement on Monday arguing that Singapore authorities caused the jams. The statement included this mystifying explanation for the jam last Saturday: a rainstorm that afternoon forced the Tanjung Puteri Customs department to switch off the electrical supply to computers and stop work temporarily. This, it said, resulted in 'more than two hours of waiting to decide whether to switch on the power supply or work manually'. The result: a 1,000-long tailback of lorries, which extended the length of the Causeway and beyond, right up to the Bukit Timah Expressway.

This week, Johor's Road Transport Department got into the act. It decided that lorries leaving the Johor Customs checkpoint should be diverted to the nearby Larkin stadium for further checks to make sure that they abided by the rules in their permits to operate lorries – for safety reasons, of course. Even the JCCC was prompted to protest against this action, rapping the department for its 'sudden' decision to check the lorries, saying that it saw 'no reason to enforce the law at that particular time and place without regard to the thousands of lorries caught in the massive traffic jams along the Causeway'.

What next, I wonder. Perhaps Johor's health department might decide that the lorry drivers, exhausted by hours of waiting, with scarcely anywhere to eat, sleep or even pee, should be subjected to a medical checkup to ensure that they are in a fit state to take to Malaysia's highways. In the interest of the safety of other motorists, of course. Meanwhile, one Malaysian minister assures her Singaporean counterpart that she has alerted the Customs department about the sorry lorry situation and it is 'making the necessary responses to ease the jam'. Nearly a week later, officials from the department say they 'have no information' about Singapore's call for urgent action to deal with the lingering lorry jam.

The message from this Malaysian comedy of errors should be clear. But in case it was not, and some Singaporeans harboured hazy ideas that the jams will disappear when the new second link to Johor opens next year, they were disabused of such foolish notions by Johor Customs officials. Yes, the second causeway will open in January. But not the checkpoint for lorries, which will be delayed because of a manpower shortage, they disclosed. Now, why the two countries spent M$1.6 billion to build the 2 km second link, touted to have a capacity of 200,000 vehicles a day, when Johor is unable to find the men to man it, is puzzling. And just why anyone should take seriously Johor's proposals for a third and fourth connection, when manpower might just evaporate when needed to operate these when they are ready, is still more baffling indeed.

Furthermore, the much vaunted Johor-Singapore-Riau Growth Triangle, premised on the hopeful belief that the three sides could work together for mutual benefit, now looks hopelessly misaligned.

Despite the daily tailbacks, extending all the way to a major expressway here and clogging up the Woodlands area as well, newspapers on this side of the Causeway have been rapped by some Malaysian politicians for highlighting the lorry snarl-ups. We should be quiet and allow the problem to be settled in the Asean spirit, they say. No, thank you.

Yet, in the spirit of neighbourliness, here is a simple solution, off the top of my head, to the lingering Causeway crawl. It is so simple that it might just appeal to those politicians with a penchant for simplistic answers to difficult questions. Such are the men who believe that a currency crisis can be corrected by chasing conspiratorial ghosts, or ports promoted by twisting exporters' arms. To such minds, rational economic arguments that value might yet be added to Malaysian exports if they can be shipped from elsewhere faster and cheaper are likely to have a suspicious ring.

But I digress. What's my solution? you ask with the patience of one who has endured a traffic jam for too long. Well, it is this: turn the Causeway into an 'all lorry' linkway, by increasing the number of lorry lanes to three. As simple as that. Already, the number of lorry lanes has been upped from one to two by Singapore authorities, leaving just one remaining lane for cars and other vehicles. But obviously, this is not enough. Recent weeks have seen scary scenes of cars and motorcycles fighting for space with lorries, which do not stick to their lanes. It has also resulted in those hoping to travel to Malaysia – tourists and day-trippers or workers returning home – having to brave massive jams.

A 'lorries only' Causeway will put an end to all that and have the following advantages. First, it will give priority to lorries carrying goods to and from Malaysia, allowing the Causeway to fulfil its primary role as an economic linkway between the two countries. Or, as Automobile Association of Singapore chief Gerard Ee puts it, 'The Causeway is an economic lifeline – free it up for those who must use it for trade, or are rushing back to see sick family, or bringing in perishable goods.' So in place of the confusing proposal by the joint Singapore-Johor committee for certain roads to be designated for empty or laden lorries, and others for cars and motorcycles, there should be a simple rule: all roads to Johor are for lorries. In one grand swoop, my suggestion will put an end to other motorists having to endure long jams at the Causeway, simply because they will not be allowed to use it, for the time being.

This will also be an act of neighbourliness. Since Singaporean travellers will not be heading to Johor to shop or patronise its nightspots, it should end the incessant complaints from Johor residents about Singaporeans raiding their supermarkets and raising the prices of food and other goodies. There will even be no need to waste precious time and effort on Goods and Services Tax checks on cars returning to Singapore, since none would have gone in the first place. No doubt, this will put some Singaporeans out. But with shopping outlets such as Carrefour and Tops having just opened here, there should be enough to keep those tireless bargain hunters busy at home for a while. Singaporeans who do need to travel to Malaysia on business or to visit family might go by train, or by air. The lower value of the ringgit has made such trips to Malaysia less expensive and so should remain within the means of most of those who could afford to travel north by car, Singapore's most costly mode of transport.

Mind you, I am not proposing that this 'all lorry' Causeway be made a permanent arrangement. Cutting off a vital link, both economic and social, between the two countries cannot be good for building ties between them. No, let it last for only as long as Malaysian officials need to put an end to the present sorry saga.

(First published 25 October 1997)

179

Malaysia's intransigence over the water issue had one unintended effect: it galvanised Singapore public opinion behind the idea that something needed to be done to 'solve' the country's longstanding dependence on Malaysia for water, even if it meant spending billions on expensive desalination and recycling technology.

Big thirst for water solution

WORLD WATER Day, March 22, passed without a splash here. This, despite Singapore being ranked the sixth most water-short country in the world and the region being plunged into one of its worst water shortages ever. Reports have been gushing from across the Causeway of droughts prompting water rationing in the Klang Valley. This has led Malaysian Prime Minister Mahathir Mohamad to declare that the water situation there was 'becoming increasingly critical'.

The timing of these developments seems unfortunate, even somewhat uncanny, given that officials from Singapore and Malaysia will meet in Kuala Lumpur this week to discuss a new bilateral water pact. This follows from Dr Mahathir's undertaking in February to supply water to Singapore ('on terms and conditions to be agreed upon') beyond 2061, when existing water agreements expire.

The catch? The Malaysian leader said he needed 60 days to get the backing of state authorities for his pledge, since water was under state, and not federal, control. He also turned down a Singapore request to settle the details of the agreement, such as how much water would be supplied and under what conditions. Such an agreement, Singapore leaders have said, would remove a major 'psychological barrier' between the two countries and replace it with a new framework of cooperation for mutual benefit. But the Malaysian prime minister told reporters he 'was not competent' to enter into such an agreement. He added too that a study on Malaysia's future water needs had been done, a significant development since the supply of water to Singapore had always been conditioned on Malaysia having enough for itself. Yet, the study has never seen the light of day.

The 60-day grace period for the agreement to be confirmed will be up in mid-April. So news on whether or not there is to be an agreement is likely to come soon after officials meet in KL 'on or around April 9' to thrash out the undertaking. Meanwhile, temperatures here continue to rise while water levels in reservoirs fall in the face of the unrelenting hot and dry spell. Demand for water has also been shooting up. It's enough to leave you feeling more than a little hot and bothered.

At such times, one might be forgiven for asking why, in island Singapore, water supply should be so dependent on the rains, or even more unpredictable foreign sources. Cannot more be done to boost the domestic supply and cut demand to reduce the country's dependence and vulnerability to water pressure from elsewhere? The thirst for a solution is all the more urgent given that water usage here continues to rise year on year – it went up by 5.2 per cent last July to 264.8 million gallons a day (mgd), roughly enough to fill 545 Olympic-sized swimming pools, compared to a daily average of 253.3 mgd in 1996.

Singapore' 14 reservoirs now provide 150 mgd, about half of the water used daily. Already, about half the available land here is used as water catchment areas and experts say that practically all domestic supplies of water have been exhausted. Further, projections by Unicef published on World Water Day also showed that, by 2025, two-thirds of the world, including many Asian countries, might be short of water. Given these portentous dark clouds on the horizon, and the possibility that the 'terms and conditions to be negotiated' may prove unpalatable, should not efforts be speeded up to forestall a future water crisis?

Some possibilities:

❖ RECYCLE, RE-USE. Of the 270 million gallons that are used daily, some 220 million gallons of waste water flow down the drains. Only about 70,000 cubic metres are treated for industrial use daily. The reason for this, ironically, might be the low cost of fresh water, leaving industries with little incentive to turn to other types of water. Raising the relative price of clean water, or offering other financial incentives for industries to use recycled water, might cut down the volume of fresh water needed each day.

❖ MAKE WATER. Plans for desalinating seawater, of which there is abundant supply all round the island, have been on the table for several years now. But it was only last year that studies were completed and a decision taken to push ahead with the project. A $1 billion plant will be built in Tuas to produce 30 million gallons of water a day. It will, however, be ready only in 2003.

Cost, it seems, rather than the lack of knowhow, is the reason the authorities chose to proceed with caution. Apart from the initial investment, it is estimated that the cost of producing a cubic metre of desalinated water is $3–3.50, about seven or eight times the cost of treating fresh water now. Assuming that Singapore's water demand stays at the current 270 mgd and domestic supply remains at 150 mgd, four of such distillation plants will be needed to make up the remaining 120 mgd. This would cost a total of $4 billion. Yet, this is less than the $5 billion being spent to build the Northeast MRT line or the planned underground road system, and a quarter of the $20 billion set aside for the Housing Board's Main Upgrading Programme to spruce up older HDB estates. Indeed, if Singapore could invest millions to develop and pioneer technology for its Electronic Road Pricing system to ensure that highways in the land-scarce country remain unclogged, why baulk at spending to develop the means to overcome its lack of an even more critical resource – water?

Sure, the cost of desalinating water will be high. But the experience of operating desalination technology could prove invaluable in the future, when alternative sources dry up. Technology also has its own payback – the more we know about desalination, the better we might be able to harness it. So, might there not be wisdom in pressing full steam ahead with desalination?

❖ EXPLORE NOVEL IDEAS. Singapore has the resources to lead the way in coming up with novel solutions to its lack of water, just as it has dared to pioneer the way in other fields. A National University of Singapore researcher, Adriel Yap, threw up some interesting ideas in a thesis published in 1995. These include having reservoirs in the sea. Linking the two ends of Pulau Ubin with the mainland would create a large enclosure that could store about 25 per cent of the rain falling on Singapore. The idea was first mooted in the late 1960s and 1970s and was found to be technically feasible, he argued. Water might also be stored in large underground tunnels or imported from water-rich countries using large water tankers, he suggested. Sounds farfetched? Well, so did the idea that man could one day drink water from the sea.

❖ DON'T WASTE. Ultimately, all efforts to boost supply will prove futile if the growth in water usage is not curbed. Steps will have to be taken to get Singaporeans to realise the strategic significance of water, including raising the water rates, penalising water wasters and getting people here used to the idea that the precious liquid does not come cheap.

Singaporeans will have to live with their lack of resources. Thankfully, ways have always been found around these constraints. When land was scarce, it was reclaimed. When highways were clogged, in came road pricing. If Singaporeans need water, they may just have to make it.

Indeed, the irony of the situation is this: the less Singapore is seen by its neighbours to be in need of water, the more likely are supplies to continue flowing on reasonable terms, rather than leaving the waters rushing inexorably out to sea.

(First published 4 April 1998)

Back from virtual reality

America in the late 1990s was a thriving and exciting place to be. The economy was booming, pushed forward by relentless spurts of technological genius. The country bestrode the world and the world seemed at peace. America was optimistic and confident, almost to a fault. Young students dreamed of becoming instant millionaires, and not a few quit school to do so. People mocked the presidential candidates who had begun making the rounds. Some said it did not matter who became president; the country would thrive regardless, almost in spite of government. Politics was 'uncool' and public service for fools. In a globalised world, these ideas spread rapidly. Dot.com fever gripped Singapore, even as dress-down Fridays hit Shenton Way. Young people here picked up the politics-is-boring-I'm-a-global-citizen-who-needs-the-state mantra.

Then came September 11. It took a painful, devastating tragedy to remind Americans – and the rest of us – of some home truths. That social cohesion matters. That it matters whom you elect president or appoint to public office. That it still matters which country you belong to, and which passport you carry. That the police, security forces and military have a job to do even when there seems to be no apparent threat. That rights need to be balanced with responsibilities, and might sometimes be curbed for the collective good. That jobs don't come easy, and employment today is no promise of plenty tomorrow.

(From 'Did the September 11 attacks change the world?'
29 September 2001, see page 196)

Chapter 7
As the world turns

THE SUN was setting on the lush Istana lawn. About 50 journalists were gathering at the gates. Some were running late, having been held up by the massive traffic snarl caused by the closure of the Central Expressway. Security guards, some Singaporean, others American, were scurrying around with furrowed brows, inspecting cars and camera equipment. The occasion was the 15-hour sleepover in Singapore by US President George W. Bush, as part of his frenzied six-nation-in-six-days swing through Asia. I was one of the Singapore journalists who had been invited for a 'media encounter' with Mr Bush. We were told to arrive by 6:30 p.m. for security clearance, more than two hours before the brief encounter with the world's most powerful man, which would last no more than a few minutes.

When the moment finally arrived, we were ushered up to the stately East Drawing Room on the second floor of the main Istana building. The doors swung open to reveal a large ornate room, with sparkling crystal chandeliers, regal gold drapery and bouquets upon bouquets of fresh tropical flowers all round. Seated in a horseshoe around the room were about a dozen leaders from the United States and Singapore, who were in the midst of closed-door but seemingly open-minded discussion. There were smiles all round, on the faces of Prime Minister Goh Chok Tong, his deputy Lee Hsien Loong, ambassador Chan Heng Chee, President Bush, US National Security Adviser Condolezza Rice, among others.

Amid the flashing of lights and jostling of frantic cameramen, Mr Goh began to speak, welcoming his guests to Singapore, before asking Mr Bush if he would like to say a few words. The American President was in an ebullient mood, declaring in Texan frankness his respect for Singapore – 'a magnificent country' – and his strong personal relations with 'my friend' Mr Goh. Then he reached out, grasped the prime minister's hand and beamed, as a hundred flashbulbs flickered.

As I surveyed the scene – the dozens of reporters from around the world, the legions of security personnel anxiously talking into communications devices in their sleeves and fingering their earpieces, the harried staffers hovering in the wings, wondering about ever more work coming their way as a result of the talks, the excited chefs and waiters bracing for the moment of truth when the party would adjourn for the dinner they had been slaving over all afternoon – I marvelled at the trouble Mr Bush and his White House team had taken to be in Singapore and Asia, albeit ever so fleetingly. He need not have come. His security chiefs had begged him not to risk making a trip to terrorist-infested Asia, which they dubbed 'a trip from Al Qaeda hell'. But he had brushed them aside with a determined 'we are going!' In his mind, it was clear: he was going to make the journey to thank his friends for having stood by America – and him – during the Iraq war, and to urge them to stay the course for the long battle ahead in his war against terror wherever it might be found, which had become the *raison d'être* of the Bush administration.

Mr Bush's warm, even effusive, remarks towards Singapore and its leaders – 'we respect Singapore people, we respect the Singapore government' – signalled a major change in the way American leaders regard Singapore and its government. But will this 'proud-to-call-them-friend' bonhomie last? Or will it pass when the political mood turns in the United States?

The question bears asking because not so long ago Singapore was viewed rather differently in Washington circles. Indeed, I recall covering Mr Goh's visit to the United States and Mexico in 1997. He stopped in Los Angeles, Chicago and New York but skipped Washington D.C. There was no meeting in the White House, let alone an invitation to stay at Blair House, the official residence reserved for special friends. Then American President Bill Clinton seemed wary of being seen with the head of a regime that had caned – 'whipped' is the word used in the US media – an American lad called Michael Fay for vandalism.

Matters got worse in the late 1990s when Singapore leaders began to be seen as champions of the 'Asian way' and 'Asian values', which many commentators viewed as being opposed to the cherished liberal values of the West. The result: Just about anything Singapore did or said came to be viewed through a rather skewed lens – that of an authoritarian state, which did not quite 'get it' ('it' being the American worldview).

This negative view of Singapore became evident to me when I spent a year in Boston in 2000. I encountered university professors who likened Singapore's early efforts to grapple with the issues raised by the emerging Internet to those by China's communists or Iran's mullahs to block the flow of information to their citizens. I tried hard to explain to them that Singapore's approach was a more nuanced 'open the windows but deal with the flies' one, but am uncertain if I convinced them. Indeed, how they could liken the actions of Singapore's then Information and the Arts Minister George Yeo – himself a Harvard alumnus – to that of a communist or a mullah was beyond me. Some academics confided privately that while they might agree with much of Singapore's policy initiatives, it was not 'appropriate' to be seen to be too effusive towards a government that was only 'partially democratic' at best.

This jaundiced view of Singapore was widespread even among ordinary Americans. One day, as I was paying for a purchase at a department store, a salesman noticed my Singapore credit card and declared with a hint of horror, 'Singapore? What's it like there? You cane people for chewing gum, don't you? You get fined for jaywalking?'

On another occasion, I drove around Boston one Sunday afternoon trying to buy a bottle of wine to take to a picnic. All the liquor stores were closed, and even supermarkets put fishnets or chains around their wine racks. American friends explained nonchalantly to me that this was part of their Puritan heritage, which frowned on the drinking of alcohol, especially on the Sabbath. In any case, it was an offence to consume alcohol in certain public places, a measure adopted to curb drunkenness on the streets, they added.

Now what if the Singapore government announced that the sale of wine would be banned on Sundays and that alcohol could not be consumed in public places? Imagine the shock and horror this would provoke and the gleeful headlines that would be spun: 'Nanny state goes dry', 'Singapore's authoritarian government bans booze'.

Those were precisely the kinds of stories and headlines that hit American newspapers in January 1992, when Singapore imposed a ban on chewing gum. The announcement of the ban came on 3 January 1992, the very day that the first President George Bush arrived for the first-ever visit to Singapore by an American president. As always, he brought with him a planeload of White House correspondents, eager for a story to send home. Guess what these reporters filed home that day, especially since the talks between US and Singapore leaders were pretty humdrum, given the lack of any pressing bilateral issues. 'Singapore – gee whiz – bans bubble gum!' Now, how's that for bad timing? an American official asked me a few days ahead of the visit by the second President Bush, hoping perhaps that Singapore was not about to commit another public relations disaster.

Singapore, as Americans would say, had a massive image problem. Unless something was done to change the way the country and its government were viewed, it would have an uphill task in any initiative it chose to pursue, be it boosting cultural links or pursuing free trade agreements. Troubled by this, I raised this theory with just about every government leader and official I happened to encounter at that time. Their response was consistent: 'Yes, we know' or 'We are working on it.'

Indeed, they seemed to be. Every minister who passed through a major American city made it a point to meet what were called 'opinion multipliers' such as politicians, editors and business leaders – people who could help shape the way Singapore was viewed. More recently, organisations such as the Singapore International Foundation, Contact Singapore and the Information and the Arts Ministry have been bringing Congressional aides, journalists and others from the United States and elsewhere to the Republic. The brief: Let them see Singapore for themselves. Let them meet Singaporeans – ministers, civil servants, businessmen, reporters, young people – whomever they wanted. As part of this programme, several groups of aides to leading American Congressmen have visited *The Straits Times* newsroom this year to find out how journalists operate in this country, with its tough – 'draconian' is the word they use – media and libel laws.

These efforts, I believe, are paying off. Putting a human face to the preconceptions that Americans have of Singapore has helped to dispel, to some extent, the dubious 'Disneyland with the death penalty' image that the country has been saddled with. When no less than Goh Chok Tong spoke out in support of bar-top dancing and allowing reverse bungee jumping, and government committees announced plans to relax censorship rules, the international media took note. Instead of 'dull and dreary' or 'safe but staid', they began to describe the city-state as 'hip and happening'. In a special report on Asian boomtowns in September 2003, *Newsweek* called Singapore 'The City that could' and lauded its 'can do' spirit in tackling all manner of problems, from traffic congestion to the Sars outbreak. Evidently, the decisive and effective manner in which the authorities in Singapore responded to the threats of terrorism and the Sars outbreak – marshalling resources and taking action at home, while quietly rallying its neighbours to do likewise – did not go unnoticed by business and political leaders abroad.

More importantly, the dramatic turnaround in American attitudes towards Singapore stems more from the changes that America has gone through after the wrenching events of 11 September 2001. The old liberal attitudes to the world, with the emphasis on upholding human rights and democracy, have been supplanted by the neo-conservative worldview, the political fashion of the times. Neo-conservatives have been likened to 'lapsed liberals' or even 'liberals who have been mugged'. It is a flippant but not inaccurate characterisation. Having been subjected to an attack has stripped them of some of their wide-eyed notions of the ways of the world.

Hence, rather than being pilloried for detaining terrorists without trial to contain the terror threat, the United States applauded Singapore's firm actions. Instead of beating the liberal drums over the tough measures taken here to tackle Sars, again Americans have cheered us on. Singapore's forthright statements in support of the war against terror and Iraq also warmed American hearts. They welcomed our candour and willingness to stand by them in a time of need.

It is not always easy to be a friend of the United States, not least in our part of the world. The appalling pictures of prisoner abuse by some American servicemen at the Abu Ghraib prison, the intelligence failures that led to no weapons of mass destruction being found, have raised grave doubts about the wisdom of the American-led push into Iraq and its dream of bringing American-style democracy to the Middle East. The continuing stalemate over the Israeli-Palestinian issue also stokes much anger towards the United States. Inevitably, questions have been raised about the price that Singapore might pay for being seen to be so staunch a supporter of the United States and its policies.

The best answer to these critics I have heard came from Singapore's ambassador to the United States, the astute Professor Chan. She said, 'In real politics, that happens – whether you articulate it or not. When major powers lobby you, they make it very clear that some of your interests could be jeopardised if you do not support them. This goes on. It is not just the United States. I was not born yesterday.'

As a small state in a turbulent neighbourhood, Singapore has learnt that it is in its interest to accept the world as it finds it, not try to wish away the political and strategic realities of the day. Nor will it bend to pressures from the outside – from countries near or far, big or small. Whether trying to keep the United States engaged in Asia, promoting the idea of free trade agreements, or facing up to the China challenge, little good comes from railing against the prevailing world order or lamenting the ways of the world. Instead, Singapore works with what it finds, engaging the powers that be, seizing opportunities as they arise, and striving to make – and influence – as many friends as possible, the more powerful the better, so long as doing so is in its national interests. Along the way, it has earned a precious reputation for effectiveness, reflected in its readiness to take bold actions when necessary and delivering on its word. This hardheaded, say-what-you-mean and do-what-you-say approach has won Singapore influence and respect abroad, beyond anything anyone might expect of a little red dot on the map.

The September 11 terrorist attacks on America shook the world, including Singapore, jolting it back to reality from the heady heights of the dot.com boom times and its virtual realities. It gave rise to banner headlines declaring that the world had changed with that era-making event. There was some truth to this, judging by the reaction of the Bush administration, which emerged from the horror as a war administration. But the media hyperbole went overboard. Some underlying realities of world politics remain.

Did the September 11 attacks change the world?

I AWOKE one cold and dreary December morning to find a strange headline in the *Boston Globe*. It declared that the Space Needle in Seattle, a famous tourist lookout over that cheery city, had been closed. It was December 1999. The big Millennium party that had been planned in Seattle was called off. No explanation was given for the surprising move, although there was some speculation of a terrorist threat. A few days later came reports that terrorist suspects had been stopped at the border between the United States and Canada. Again, there was speculation that they were out to mar the dawn of the new century with devilish destruction. Most people shrugged it off and went about their business. My wife and I flew to New York to spend Christmas. The flight took no more than an hour and we always marvelled at how hassle-free such domestic flights were. Passengers strolled into the airport's domestic lounge a few minutes before takeoff, as free and easy as if taking a bus ride.

As 31 December 1999 drew nearer, reports surfaced of a planned massive terrorist attack in New York on New Year's Eve. Still, huge crowds filled Times Square, blasé about the threats. January 1 came and went – thankfully – without incident. Before long, fears about terrorism faded away, seemingly as over-hyped as the much-dreaded millennium bug. People went back to the ski slopes, back to school, back to work. Life returned to normal. It was a happy time. This was the carefree world my wife and I experienced.

America in the late 1990s was a thriving and exciting place to be. The economy was booming, pushed forward by relentless spurts of technological genius. The country bestrode the world and the world seemed at peace. America was optimistic and confident, almost to a fault. Young students dreamed of becoming instant millionaires, and not a few quit school to do so. People mocked the presidential candidates who had begun making the rounds. Some said it did not matter who became president; the country would thrive regardless, almost in spite of government. Politics was 'uncool' and public service for fools. Newspapers ran reports of students from public policy schools rushing to join their business school counterparts in signing up with private firms like Microsoft and Goldman Sachs, not the Foreign Service or Treasury. Little wonder, since Washington was besieged by partisan deadlock. Political news was dominated by sex scandals and leaks about other shenanigans.

Perhaps the silliest manifestation of the spirit of the times was the 'dress down' culture that took hold in offices, with professionals discarding their suits and ties for California-style bermudas and tees at work. How this gave a boost to productivity was a mystery.

IN A globalised world, these ideas spread rapidly. Dot.com fever gripped Singapore, even as dress down Fridays hit Shenton Way. Young people here picked up the politics-is-boring-I'm-a-global-citizen-who-needs-the-state mantra, which had become chic wherever the Internet or MTV was found. There was much talk of wanting to be their own bosses, yearning to see the world, never coming home. Even signs that the economy might be headed for another downturn did not cause much alarm. Government calls for restraint and scenarios of a looming economic Everest ahead were shrugged off. With a general election round the corner, many expected that the politicians would soon dole out goodies galore and all would be well.

Then came September 11.

The searing images of hijacked planes crashing into the World Trade Center and the Pentagon were enough to cause all signs of past 'irrational exuberance' to evaporate. The world woke up the next day and found a different world. Francis Fukuyama, an American professor of international political economy, summed up this transformation best when he wrote:

> 'The long economic boom of the Clinton years and America's easy dominance of world politics have allowed Americans to wallow in such self-indulgent behaviour as political scandal and identity politics, or partisanship that has grown more strident as the underlying issues narrowed. Many Americans lost interest in public affairs, and in the larger world beyond its borders; others expressed growing contempt for government. This was nowhere truer than in the world of high-tech and finance, where a kind of techno-libertarianism took hold in the 1990s. The government, according to this view, contributed nothing useful and stood in the way of true "value creators".

The nation state was said to be obsolete ... the apostles of the new economy declared the irrelevance of everything invented before the Internet, and of any skills other than their own.

'I was shocked when a portfolio-manager friend told me a while back that he was seriously considering renouncing his American citizenship and moving to the Bahamas to avoid paying US taxes. In this respect, the September 11 attacks on Wall Street were a salutary lesson. The weightlessness of the new economy will not protect you from falling concrete; Microsoft and Goldman Sachs will not send aircraft carriers and F-16s to the Gulf to track down Osama bin Laden; only the military will. The 1990s saw the social and economic gulf widen between the Harvard- and Stanford-educated investment bankers, lawyers and software engineers who worked in those twin towers, and the blue-collar workers who went to their rescue. This shared victimisation powerfully reminds Americans that they are all, in the end, mutually dependent members of the same community.'

It took a painful, devastating tragedy to remind Americans – and the rest of us – of some home truths. That, corny as it may sound, life is as fragile as it is precious, and families and friends matter, in good times as in bad. That social cohesion across classes and races matters, and widening wage gaps between these groups cannot be shrugged off as the will of the market. That it matters who you elect as president or prime minister and appoint to public office, to ensure that the country is in good hands, not least when the going gets tough out of the blue. That it still matters which country you belong to, and which passport you carry. That the police, security forces and military have a job to do even when there seems to be no apparent threat. That rights need to be balanced with responsibilities, and might sometimes be curbed for the collective good. That jobs don't come easy, and employment today is no promise of plenty tomorrow. That millionaires are not made out of nothing. Sure, the dot.com bubble had already burst and the US economy was teetering on the brink even before the terrorists struck. But suddenly, as the world reeled in shock at the attacks, everything seemed so much clearer.

It is this, I think, that commentators mean when they say glibly that the 'world changed' after September 11. As Americans rally round their president, politicians put aside their bickering and the people brace themselves for the sacrifices that a long-drawn-out war on terrorism will entail. The dreamy, happy-go-lucky, somewhat unreal spirit of the late 1990s has given way to a new, more sombre and ultimately perhaps more realistic mood. Call it the end of the 'new economy folly'.

IN ITS wake is a period of great uncertainty. There will be testing times ahead – politically, economically and strategically. An engaged and enraged America portends a new period, which will be shaped, in the short term, by the ways in which the world responds to the terrorist attacks. But that, really, is as far as it goes. No one should fall for the new media babble that the 'world has changed forever'. It is simply way too early to foretell how things will shape up, or if any of the short-term reactions will have lasting effects. In all likelihood, in the longer term, the twists and turns of life will continue, and much of the underlying truths about human nature, societies and international relations in the world of realpolitik will apply.

No, the terrorist attacks did not remake the world. To say that would be to give them too much credit. Rather, the horror of their deeds jolted people back to the real world, with all its complexities and challenges.

I have dwelt at length on this because, in truth, just about everything above applies closer to home. Singaporeans will do well to ponder the events of September 11, and the lessons that might be drawn from them. Even as they do, they should not lose sight of the longer-term challenges that have been looming – the need to find new economic niches and tap emerging markets, to find new jobs for older workers, grapple with the rapidly ageing society and declining birth rates, as well as the perennial necessity of good race relations. These remain and are perhaps all the more urgent now.

(First published 29 September 2001)

The story of how Singapore came to be the first Asian country to sign a free trade deal with the United States begins with an unlikely tale of midnight talks over a golf game that nearly never happened, and a visit to a factory in Mexico. Goh Chok Tong seized the day, or night, when he persuaded President Bill Clinton to take a shot at a trade deal with Singapore.

Taking a midnight swing for free trade

IT WAS at a factory in Guadalajara in western Mexico, back in September 1997, when I first heard the audacious suggestion that perhaps, someday, Singapore might sign a free trade agreement with the United States. The event was a visit by Goh Chok Tong to Mexico, where he was opening a new US$11 million plant for NatSteel Electronics to produce electronic gadgets.

The question on everyone's minds: What had made a Singapore firm decide to set up a plant in Guadalajara? Why not Geylang or Ghim Moh? Or even Batam or Suzhou?

The word on everyone's lips: Nafta.

Referring to the North American Free Trade Agreement (Nafta) between the United States, Mexico and Canada, company officials explained that the lower tariffs under Nafta made Mexico an attractive location for companies which export mainly to the United States. Japanese, Korean and firms from other nations had flocked to Mexico.

Then came the suggestion: Perhaps someday Singapore might sign an FTA with the United States.

I recall polite laughter and smiles all round at the idea, almost as if someone had suggested that Singapore should hitch itself to a giant tugboat to be towed to a friendlier and more dynamic region. Just a few days earlier, Mr Goh had made a speech at an official reception in which he revived an idea he had mooted for a link between Nafta and the Asean Free Trade Agreement. Perhaps that was considered a more likely prospect than a US-Singapore deal. After all, in the early 1990s, he had said that Singapore would be willing to accept an invitation to join Nafta, since the United States was its major market. But alas, the call never came.

Not until one rainy night in November 2000, when Mr Goh asked then President Bill Clinton for a midnight round of golf, while both leaders were attending an Apec meeting in Brunei. It was to be a rematch of a game they had had in Canada in 1998. Rain nearly led to the game being called off, but thankfully, the avid golfers persisted. Sometime that night, it seems, the idea for a US-Singapore deal took flight. Soon afterwards, both leaders announced that talks would begin on a bilateral trade pact, the first of its sort between the United States and an Asian country. The FTA signing ceremony marked the culmination of a frenzied two years of negotiations.

Little wonder there were smiles all round, given the lightning speed at which this complex agreement had been reached, despite a change of US leadership following the 2000 election which saw George W. Bush assuming the presidency. At stake are thousands of jobs and over $200 million a year in cost savings for Singapore firms exporting to the United States, Singapore's second largest export market. American companies account for more than half of Singapore's exports to the United States, and Singapore is the 12th largest trading partner of the United States, with 'only a few European countries being larger markets for the US', as US ambassador to Singapore

Frank Lavin noted recently. Lower tariffs will mean lower costs for Singapore firms exporting to the United States, while the opening of markets will help draw more US firms here, bringing in investment and jobs as well as lower prices for some US goods. American companies offering their services could also force a shake-up in some industries such as banking, giving local players a wake-up call to deliver better quality services.

Beyond this, the FTA also addresses a 'hidden agenda' that has been a concern of Singapore's leaders for decades – how to keep the United States engaged in this part of the world. As Trade and Industry Minister George Yeo said last month, the trade pact binds not just Singapore but also Southeast Asia closer to the United States economically and politically, and 'helps anchor the US in Asean'.

Undoubtedly, yesterday's signing ceremony marked a high point in Singapore-US ties. It is no exaggeration to say that ties have never been better. Indeed, they have been worse; there was a definite cooling in the mid-1990s after the Michael Fay episode and when, rightly or wrongly, the view took hold in Washington that Singapore was championing an illiberal line in the debate over whether Asian societies were culturally disposed to democracy.

Actions speak louder than words. And it is Singapore's strong stance and firm actions in the post-September 11 fight against terrorism, as well as the war against Iraq, which have won it friends and favour in Washington. Robert Bauerlein, vice-president of the Boeing Company, who co-chairs the Singapore caucus in Washington, summed it up this way: 'Singapore has stepped up to the plate and taken on the big issues, first after 9-11, then over Iraq, and now with Sars.'

The result has been a readiness in Washington to recognise Singapore's efforts, as evidenced by the red carpet treatment at the White House given to Mr Goh and his team. This is how Mr Bush put it when he met Mr Goh at the White House in May 2003: 'The prime minister is a man with whom I enjoy good conversations. He's got good advice, and I'm proud to call him friend.'

Mr Bush is widely known to be a man who values his friends. In today's world, it is in Singapore's interests to have him count Mr Goh and the Republic as friends.

(First published 8 May 2003)

The rise of China will pose both problems and opportunities for Singapore, like everyone else. But there's no avoiding it. How it turns out depends on how companies and citizens play the China card.

Bracing for the China challenge

THEY call it the China challenge. It is big, it is looming, and it could change life as we know it. Trade and Industry Minister George Yeo pointed to the challenge ahead in a riveting speech in Parliament in July 2001. The vision of the emerging China he painted was at once both thrilling and terrifying.

For even while Brigadier-General (NS) Yeo told Singaporeans to get ready their skateboards and prepare to latch onto economic opportunities as the China juggernaut gathers speed, he also noted how Taiwanese companies were fleeing to the mainland in search of lower costs and bigger markets, giving rise to a palpable 'hissing' sound like so much air rushing out of a deflating balloon.

For in reality the China challenge is twofold: How to stay ahead of the competition that is as eager to get a piece of the action in the growing China market, while preventing a rush away from the domestic economy, leaving it bereft of investments and jobs. This two-pronged challenge has been exercising minds, both here and abroad, in recent months. Government officials here have been bullish about developments in China for some time. They are not alone. China has been hogging the headlines of leading business and news magazines for weeks. The accounts tell the same story of a rapidly rising economy.

But it is the sheer scale of the economic and social transformation under way that is breathtaking.

Consider a *Time* magazine report of 23 July 2001, which noted that Motorola had spent US$1.9 billion (S$3.4 billion) on a semiconductor plant in Tianjin last year – more than what it had invested in Malaysia over the past three decades. 'Assuming nations in the region don't orchestrate a turnaround soon, the current slump might provide China with an opportunity to steal the show. Many foreign investors already shun Southeast Asian nations in favour of China's huge market and cheap manpower,' the report said.

A simple table published in *Businessweek* highlighted the scale of the competitive advantage enjoyed by China. Office rentals in prime sites in Hongkong are more than three times that in Shanghai. A businessman might hire a personal assistant for US$3,500 a month in Hongkong. He could get seven assistants for the same amount in Shanghai. Getting a geomancer to invoke the gods to look favourably on his company's premises would cost 50 US cents per square foot in Hongkong. In Shanghai, the gods could be similarly swayed for just six cents.

Given these numbers, it is little wonder that Hongkong apparel maker Giordano has decided to base its international IT operations in Guangzhou. But it was not just lower costs that beckoned. As Giordano's president Peter Lau told *Businessweek*, 'We've found this team much more effective than the previous setup in Hongkong. I suppose it is the devotion to their work, as opposed to the Hongkong staff, whose focus was almost entirely on short-term pay.' To add insult to injury, the magazine added, 'Now Hongkong IT employees go to Guangzhou for training, a serious comedown.'

Those who still imagine that Chinese competition will be mainly in the lower-end sectors of the economy should listen to what Ian Johnston, Asia-Pacific technology director for American manufacturer Agilent Technologies, told *Asiaweek* recently about a Chinese technology company, Huawei Technologies, based in Shenzhen. He said, 'Huawei's software and R&D skills are getting much, much better. I've been telling Western companies they had better put their thinking caps on. These guys are sawing away right quick and, sooner or later, you'll just drop through the floor.'

Here comes the truly troubling bit. In each of the above accounts of lower costs, burgeoning markets and workers hungry for progress, you could just as well replace the economy being compared to China with the word 'Singapore', and a similar story would ring true. Inevitably, the cry will ring out, as it did in Parliament: What is the government going to do about it?

BG Yeo was the man with a plan, as he returned to the topic of China for the second time in two weeks. In a speech peppered with anecdotes, he explained how Singapore hoped to turn adversity to advantage, by seizing opportunities in China's emerging economy, while also 'hurrying up the value ladder' by upgrading its workers and industries. Clearly, the strategy makes much sense. Singaporeans would be fools to pass up on what could be the biggest economic opportunity of the next decade and beyond. And they would be foolhardy to ignore the risk of massive unemployment, as firms uproot and investments and jobs head for China.

In all likelihood, there will be both economic gain from projects in China, as well as pain from job losses here. Those affected by these developments will come from opposing ends of the socioeconomic spectrum. Ways will have to be found to help some of those left behind in the process. Indeed, how to walk this economic tightrope could prove one of the biggest political challenges ahead.

Nor should anyone embrace the China challenge in the blind hope that good bilateral relations or ties of ethnic affinity and knowing some Mandarin will put Singaporeans on an express lane to success in China. Indeed, while travelling with several business delegations in China, I came across many Chinese Singaporeans who confessed that they had never felt more un-Chinese than in their first forays there. For while most Singaporeans might look and speak like their mainland counterparts, a deep gulf exists in their worldview, borne of Singapore's long exposure to the West. Ask any official who has worked on the Suzhou industrial project and he will have endless tales to tell about how difficult it is to bridge this gap.

Besides, Singaporeans will not be the only ones rushing to knock on China's door. Many others have come to the same conclusion and will be doing so too. While Singaporeans' ethnic backgrounds will be an edge, it will not amount to much unless its businessmen are also swift and savvy. To win, they will have to be shrewd businessmen, not just Chinese ones.

Good businessmen know the hazards of getting carried away by straight-line extrapolations of previous forecasts that show China chalking up 7 per cent growth a year for the next five years. Sure, the long-term trends may point upwards, but there will be short-term ups and downs, varying from sector to sector. Get on the wrong side of those crucial curves, and you could lose everything. This point is worth making, at the risk of sounding like a party pooper. For while a China drive is to be encouraged, especially when all other engines of economic growth around the globe are stalling, the government should make clear that its trumpeting of China's charms is not a blank-cheque endorsement to rush in where the more astute choose not to tread. Businessmen will have to do their homework, take risks and live with them. They should not expect any bailouts at taxpayers' expense on the grounds that 'the government told me so', as some had lamented in the 1990s, when the much-touted regionalisation drive left some firms, including some government-linked ones, exposed to steep downsides.

One final proviso: Even as Singapore steps up its surge into China, it will need to assure its minority races that it is driven by purely economic considerations. This might seem patently obvious, given the government's scrupulously multiracial stand over the decades, but ethnic sentiments have a way of being stoked up for the most unpredictable of reasons. Anyone who doubts this need only be reminded of how the seemingly innocuous slogan for the Speak Mandarin campaign – 'If you are Chinese, make a statement' – once proved controversial, provoking much angst among some in the minority communities.

China beckons. Singaporeans had better brace themselves for the ride. This could prove to be exhilarating or excruciating. Or probably both. Much will depend on their ability to handle the economic and political twists and turns as the juggernaut rushes along. Hang on.

(First published 28 July 2001)

I Not Clever

Here's an idea for Jack Neo: Perhaps his next film should be called *I Not Clever*. It could feature the three boys from the first film, having grown up, only to join the thousands of junior college students seen weeping inconsolably on learning that they had scored only three A's when the A-level results are announced. Horror of horrors, what future can there be with only three A's when 1,364 students – or 12 per cent of the cohort – managed a perfect score in the A-level examinations in 2001?

(From 'Do schools suffer from A's inflation?'
16 March 2002, see page 228)

Chapter 8
Can Singapore be remade?

THE LATE 1990s and early years of the 21st century have been testing times for Singaporeans. Since the 1997 Asian financial crisis, Singaporeans have been experiencing a roller-coaster ride. From the seemingly quick recovery and the dot.com boom of the late 1990s, which was followed by the bursting of the 'irrationally exuberant' bubble, then the September 11 terrorist attacks, the Iraq war and the Sars epidemic, it has been the best and the worst of times in rapid succession. These bewildering, even traumatic, years, coming after the 'more good years' period of the 1990s, have left a deep sense of foreboding about the future among many Singaporeans, both young and old.

Many believe that the political and social system that served the country well in the past can't simply go on as it was, and there is a need for fundamental change. Given this deep-seated belief, the government's determination to Remake Singapore resonated with the people. The pledge that there would be no sacred cows, and no stone left unturned went down well and raised expectations that important questions would be asked and assumptions questioned, even if many remained cynical and wondered if indeed the process would go far enough.

Ask Singaporeans what they would like to change about their country, and you will find no shortage of views about what is wrong with Singapore society, and just what needs to be done to remake it. Indeed, as a member of the Remaking Singapore Committee (RSC), set up in 2001 and led by the then young minister of state Dr Vivian Balakrishnan, I did just that. We met Singaporeans from all segments of society, face-to-face, online, in groups large and small, to gather such views.

What struck me most about these sessions was how consistently some facets of life in Singapore keep coming up for criticism. They are raised invariably at forums such as in Parliament, community dialogues, Feedback Unit sessions, television and radio talkshows, in the Forum pages of the newspapers, or just in casual coffeeshop or dinner party talk. The issues are perennial concerns – old chestnuts if you like – which never seem to go away. Indeed, one afternoon several years ago, a Singapore 21 group, of which I was a member, drew up a list of 'push' and 'pull' factors which drove Singaporeans away or drew them back and kept them rooted to this country. After several hours of brainstorming, the list filled two large white boards. It was a familiar wishlist, which changed little when the Remaking Singapore Committee later took up the same issues.

The 'Remake this!' wishlist went something like this:

❖ **Cost of living:** Singapore is an expensive place to live in and raise a family. It seems to get more costly by the year. But what rankles most is the way some fee increases seem to hit all at the same time. This happened in the early 1990s, when various government departments moved to raise their charges, making up for having put off adjustments in the late 1980s, in the face of an economic recession. The unhappiness gave rise to the Cost Review Committee, which published its first report in 1993 to address concerns about the rising cost of living in Singapore. Similar cost pressures were felt in 2002, when a string of impending fee hikes announced about the same time – Goods and Services Tax, Housing Board carpark charges, phone charges, as well as bus and taxi fares, to name a few – sparked much unhappiness on the ground.

Two factors seem to be at work in fuelling disquiet over the multiple jumps in fees. First is what might be called the 'election effect'. Because 2001 was an election year, many government departments put cost increases on hold, only to have to play catchup after the polls. Coming all at once, who could blame people for railing at the added cost burden?

Second, explanations that government departments are merely 'recovering costs' do not satisfy anyone, since it is often unclear just how these costs are derived or even if they are justified. Hence, when former Speaker Tan Soo Khoon hit out in a speech in Parliament in 2002 at the 'Seven Wonders of Singapore', suggesting that excesses by government departments, such as their spending on splendid new five-star buildings and facilities, added to unnecessary cost increases, he struck a popular chord. Indeed, every time I visit the lavish new Foreign Affairs Ministry building in Tanglin, with its impressive hallways and soft lighting, splashing fountains, fancy paintings and sculptures, I cannot help but wonder at the expense of taxpayers' dollars. Or take the HDB Hub, with its cavernous hall where people wait in luxury for allocations of subsidised public housing amid fancy lighting and display screens, which make private developers' offices look spartan and shabby. All of this has helped frame in the public mind a picture of a profligate public sector, spending taxpayers' money freely, even while complaining about pressures on the national coffers. This image will take a long time to shake off, despite all the efforts of the new Cut Waste Committee that the government has set up.

This is a great pity. For to be fair, many of the initiatives taken by the public service reflect a well-meaning desire to meet the ever-rising expectations of the population. Take, for example, the by now infamous air-conditioned bus interchange at the HDB Hub in Toa Payoh. My first impression on encountering this was to think it was a great idea. Having had to use the smoky old facility it replaced, I saw precious little reason why bus commuters should be begrudged a comfortable journey to and from work, just like those who use private transport enjoy. To bring this point home, my colleagues and I at *The Straits Times* urged the HDB to reveal information on the new hub, how much it cost, how this would be paid for, and how it reflected public demands for such facilities. They declined, saying they would wait for the minister in charge to disclose this. That proved a fateful mistake. Before the minister could do so, Mr Tan struck with his memorable 'wonders of the world' speech and the deep impression it left was of a wasteful bureaucracy going out on a lavish limb, despite a public desire to contain costs. No amount of damage control afterwards, citing surveys to show how public feedback had pushed for such improvements, could undo the image of wanton wastefulness.

The moral of the story: every time I read about some new government service or initiative which sounds wonderful, a little voice rings out in my head with three crucial questions: How much? Who will pay? Who asked for it?

Public service providers, I think, would do well to have these three golden questions emblazoned on their walls. Each time they do their sums to argue that a new service or initiative is 'affordable', they should have at the ready clear and convincing answers to these three questions. Being 'affordable' would be necessary but not sufficient to proceed with a new initiative, which inevitably causes a ratcheting up of expectations of public services – whether it is new features like high-speed or 'talking' lifts in public housing or air-conditioned bus interchanges. An additional 'market test' of whether the public is not just able, but also willing, to pay for them is called for.

❖ **Pressure cooker schools:** Singapore students are some of the best-educated, but also seem to be among the most stressed in the world. The pressures in schools and at home to do well in examinations has turned schooldays into a drudgery for many young Singaporeans, as was movingly captured in the Jack Neo hit film *I Not Stupid*, which even Education Ministry officials have confessed to watching and empathising with. The result of these pressures: some parents have chosen to opt out of the system, and even the country.

Streaming of students at primary four, the ranking of schools, the heavy emphasis on examination grades, and the strain that the bilingual policy puts on some children, are among the chief concerns of Singapore's parents, who place much store on how their children fare in schools. Indeed, so strongly do people feel about this, that it prompted Hong Kah GRC MP Amy Khor to declare during a parliamentary debate in 2002 that streaming had caused so much public anguish that it would be 'morally irresponsible' if she did not speak up against it, while her colleague from Ang Mo Kio GRC Inderjit Singh charged that many parents, teachers and principals were secretly against streaming but feared to speak up against it.

The usual defence of the system has been that it does much better than past ones in helping the weakest students, by keeping them in school through a tailored programme which gives them skills employers want. The result has been a larger part of each year's batch of students completing 10 years of basic education and fewer dropouts along the way. This system, as such, is less 'wasteful' in that it prevents more students being 'lost' than if they were put through a uniform programme which might not suit them. Streaming, in other words, is a way to 'customise' the education system to meet the disparate needs of students. As the system evolves, the degree with which it is customised should be increased, rather than having a cookie cutter one-stream-fits-all system, the argument goes.

The cost, however, is the pressure imposed on thousands of children who are called on to prove in examinations at age 10 that they are a cut above their peers and so should not be consigned to the slow lane. These days, the pressures begin the moment they enter school, as parents fear that their children will be singled out for 'learning support' programmes, which begin as early as primary one. Such learning support programmes are well-intentioned – they aim to help students who are a little behind their peers, either because they are slower in developing or had not benefited from kindergarten classes that gave them a bit of a head start. But the result is often a ratcheting up of expectations of what children entering school are supposed to know, and with it, the steps that parents will take to give their precious little ones a leg-up in life.

This relentless drive to improve their kids' lot has caused parents and schools to place heavy emphasis on academic achievements, exams and rote learning. Today, just about everyone laments how the high-pressure system has led to the deadening of creativity and hampered development of confident, independent young minds.

Steps are being taken to correct this, including cutting curriculum content, modifying the way in which schools are ranked to make the assessment less grade-centred, and even to streamline the streaming system. These moves are certainly welcome; many would say they are long overdue. But the most critical changes unveiled, it seems to me, are those that relate to the way we test and assess our young children, and select them for places at universities and other tertiary institutions, with greater emphasis being placed on interviews and co-curricular programmes. It is these changes further upstream in the education system that will help foster the kind of thinking, questioning young minds that everyone now agrees will be needed in the working world of tomorrow. Give students incentives to do well in more than just their school work. Reward initiative and critical thinking through project work, and recognise their activities outside the classroom or school. And make all of this count towards progressing onto higher education. When parents see that the learning that goes on outside the classroom is as critical to their child's success as the teaching within, they will begin to adjust. Only then will real change come in the education system.

❖ **Bridging ethnic divides:** Despite the growing cosmopolitanisation – some would say Westernisation – of Singapore society, ethnic sentiments and concerns run deep, and surface from time to time. Concerns about preserving Singapore's ethnic cultures and roots, and the tension between doing so and fostering a 'Singaporean Singapore' simmer beneath the surface of the seemingly quiescent surface of ethnic harmony. There are also some who harbour doubts about whether the minorities are treated fairly, or subject to discrimination at work or in the marketplace for homes and other goods and services.

Every time an ethnic issue emerges, Special Assistance Plan schools take a beating, with calls going out for them to be opened up to non-Chinese students to ensure that they do not produce students who cannot identify with Singapore's multiracial ethos. Here, as with the issue of bilingualism, there remains a deep-seated English- and Chinese-educated divide. The former lament the emphasis on the mother tongue and the stress imposed on their children who struggle with Mandarin in particular. Less often heard, however, is the view of the silent majority of Chinese-educated Singaporeans, many of whom feel that the government gives in too quickly to pressures from the articulate English-educated minority. It does not do enough to support and promote the teaching and public use of the mother tongue, standards of which are falling, they charge.

In my view, there can be no resolution to this long-standing debate unless the two sides come to see that their views need to be set against the broader picture of multiracial Singapore. Ironically, Singapore needs to have strong Chinese, Indian and Malay roots to be Singapore. Undo, or overdo, that and you risk losing its unique character. A pseudo-Western Singapore, with its people neither Asian nor Western, would not be one that is comfortable with itself, let alone the rest of the world. How to preserve its ancient Asian core, while being open and receptive to new ideas, from East and West, creating its own 'Singaporean' ethos, will be a challenge that Singapore's young society will have to grapple with for many years to come.

Post-September 11, moves have been made to bring the ethnic groups closer together, following recognition at the highest levels that the divides between the races need tending in the wake of the Jemaah Islamiah terrorist arrests and the growing wave of radical Islamisation that is sweeping the world. But how close can ethnic self-help groups be, without undermining their *raison d'être*, namely the idea that Singaporeans of one race are better at reaching out and helping their own kind? Many have long disputed this assumption. To my mind, it still holds, and will do so for some time to come.

Even as we go about upholding Singapore's ethnic roots, more will have to be done to reinforce what Singaporeans share in common, without having to pretend that race has diminished as a potent force in society here. Proposals to get schoolchildren to play games and interact more in school go only so far. Far more important is what they learn at home, the values and attitudes they imbibe from their parents – you and me – about the importance of living up to the multiracial ideal which gave birth to this country.

❖ **Beyond the OB markers:** Political debate, or the lack of it, is in itself a source of much contention, ironically. Singaporeans often speak up forcefully about the fears they have over speaking up on the issues of the day. High-profile, heavy-handed put-downs by political leaders, defamation suits and retribution towards critics, have all contributed over the years to what many say is a 'chilling effect' towards open discussion of public policy. Having government leaders who are less thin-skinned and quick to shoot back would help ease public fears about speaking up, or so the argument goes. Some also want the so-called OB markers for public discussion to be more clearly defined.

No doubt, there is some truth to this. But I have often wondered if the 'fear factor' might not also be a convenient cop-out for those who would rather not take a stand and defend their views, come what may. What, I wonder, would our forefathers, who fought for their right to have their say in how the country was run, make of this collective timidity, or even indifference?

If you ask me, the OB marker debate is a bit of a red herring, a confusion caused by an overstretching of a golfing metaphor by a political elite highly enamoured with the game. Just how would the OB markers be defined? After all, the issues that are likely to cause a stir change with context and the times. Is race outside the OB markers? No, judging by how freely it is discussed these days. Should the People's Action Party and its leaders be beyond question? Certainly not; nor are they spared, not even by their own MPs these days.

Having had to navigate these OB markers as a journalist for over a decade, my sense is that any attempt to define them would not only be an exercise in futility, but also counterproductive, since it might mean restricting areas of discussion preemptively and needlessly. Instead, I would suggest a more robust approach, where Singaporeans take the government at its word when it says it welcomes more debate, and accept that thinking is indeed allowed. The more Singaporeans who take up the call to air their views, the more this will become the norm, rather than the current, lamentably pervasive 'don't quote me' syndrome.

This need not mean anarchy or an absolute free-for-all. Especially in an ethnically diverse society such as Singapore, some issues will remain sensitive, such as those related to race and religion. These will always require care when deciding when and how to discuss them. Having to find the right place, time, context, manner and tone to tackle sensitive issues is not unique to Singapore. Most societies practise care in airing certain issues at the appropriate place and time. In the United States, it has given rise to widespread political correctness on some issues, with society considering some views beyond the pale. This has sometimes taken caution too far, but it does show that even in the United States, a champion of free speech, there are some unspoken, undefined OB markers, which society recognises and accepts, adjusting and adapting them as times change.

Some, no doubt, would dismiss this view as being idealistic. I would much rather Singaporeans be idealistic and ready to live by their ideals, than apathetic and needlessly cynical about their own society. The proverbial glass can be either half empty or half full, depending on what you choose to make of it.

❖ **Not the Victorian age:** Given Singapore's more educated, widely travelled and globally exposed population, it is no wonder that some chafe at censorship restrictions that were imposed in different times. Many have pointed out inconsistencies and anomalies in censorship laws: R(A) films are shown downtown but not in the suburbs, to keep up the pretence that this keeps the heartlanders pure and proper. For commercial reasons, some movies which are rated R elsewhere get easier ratings here with cuts, leaving the young exposed to their adult themes and adults infuriated at being treated like children. Why is *Ally McBeal*, with its sometimes raunchy themes and scenes, allowed on prime time on Channel 5, while *Sex and the City* (available elsewhere in Asia) was – until recently – banned, even on late-night cable? Why did – again until recently – all videotapes and discs, even the most innocuous ones used mostly for private viewing, need to be vetted, when much more salacious content can be found freely on the Internet?

Following the electoral setback in the 1991 general elections, the government has trodden very carefully on these socio-cultural issues. It concluded that it lost ground in 1991 because the conservative heartlands reacted to what it perceived as a too-rapid move to liberalise and open up Singapore society to foreign, especially Western, influence. Aware that these HDB heartlands remain the core of its electoral base, the PAP has been careful to tend this ground. Yet, government leaders are savvy enough to know that to keep Singapore's talent at home, and draw foreign talent here as well, it will have to relax some of its controls.

The PAP's broad thinking on this issue was well articulated by BG Yeo in his 'pruning the banyan tree' speech of 1991, when he assured members of a university alumni group that change would come, over time. But given the political backdrop, any further opening up of society will have to be done gradually – a 'softly, softly', proceed quietly and at a pace that the majority is comfortable with affair, rather than any big bang relaxation of political controls. This seems sensible, but raises questions about whether the pace of change will be rapid enough in today's Internet age of fleet-footed, highly mobile workers, full of angst and attitude, and hungry to connect and engage the wider world.

CAN these aspects of Singapore society be remade without it coming unstuck? I think so. Indeed, I would go further to argue that they must be remade if Singapore is to take the next big leap to being a 'great little nation', a vision which Goh Chok Tong held out once in a speech soon after taking over as Singapore's leader.

No doubt some of the underlying realities of Singapore society will not change with a wave of a Remaking wand. Yet, given that many of these issues appear again and again on many Singaporeans' 'remake this!' wishlist, they will have to be confronted sooner or later. This will make for livelier political discourse, a messier, less ordered society, perhaps even one that is more difficult to manage and lead. But as Singapore develops and plugs into a globalised world, these changes in its politics are ineluctable. Indeed, to my mind, the risk of this needs to be set against the even greater danger of Singaporeans falling into general apathy about their country and politics. Or, just as worrying, going into 'auto pilot', with top civil servants, policy makers, academics, journalists and other bright young minds choosing the easier option of reaching for tried and tested solutions and pat answers, rather than actively thinking about the critical challenges at hand.

Put simply, thinking will not only have to be allowed, it will be utterly imperative for Singaporeans to do so if we are to find our way forward and continue to thrive in an uncertain, fast-changing world.

Education and the stresses and strains it imposes on Singapore's youth are a pressing concern among parents, judging by the large number of emails I receive every time I return to this theme. Many lament the pressures being put on their children, by schools, society – and other parents.

Do schools suffer from A's inflation?

IT WAS one of those fight-back-tears moments. Scrawny and meek, teenager Kok Pin is being caned by his mother for not doing as well in his examination as she might like.

'Why can't you study hard and concentrate?' she screams, lashing away.

'Please, ma,' he cries. 'Don't beat me anymore. I promise to get 90 marks for you next time.'

This is a vain hope, as the artistic boy is obviously struggling to pass in subjects like mathematics.

The silence in the darkened cinema hall, where the latest Jack Neo movie, *I Not Stupid*, is playing before a sellout crowd, makes it evident that the pathos of this senseless pursuit of '90 marks' is shared by many. Indeed, many know that this beat-the-grades-out-of-them scene is not just a piece of fiction in a homegrown flick. Neo's social commentary – some might say political satire – hits home precisely because the stereotypes he portrays are both funny and familiar.

There are indeed parents who do not want their children to mix with students from the EM3 stream, the slow lane for about one in five students who are deemed unable to cope with the regular curriculum. There are some teachers who whisper that students in the stream are not worth bothering over; after all, they are destined for ITE – which stands not for the Institute of Technical Education, but 'it's the end'. Such grade snobbery among students, parents and teachers exists throughout the education system, whether you are in EM3 or in the Gifted programme.

So, here's an idea for Jack: Perhaps his next film should be called *I Not Clever*. It could feature the three boys from the first film, having grown up, only to join the thousands of junior college students seen weeping inconsolably on learning that they had scored only three A's when the A-level results are announced. Horror of horrors, what future can there be with only three A's when 1,364 students – or 12 per cent of the cohort – managed a perfect score in last year's A-level examinations? At some top junior colleges, four to five in 10 bagged four A's. As if this were not enough, there were students who walked away with not just four, but nine distinctions in their A-level and Special papers.

The report of these stellar results made it to the front page of this newspaper the next morning. Predictably, irate parents telephoned our Newsline to complain: why were some junior colleges mentioned and not others, which also had students who scored A's? It's not fair, they protested, you should have featured my son or daughter's school! No amount of argument would convince them of the merits of our decision to feature not only the top students, but also to make space for the less able who had done well, despite the odds. Sigh! As Jack might say, there would not be a rat race if there were no rats prepared to chase each other's tails!

This is no laughing matter, for the relentless pressure to score A's – and many of them – gives rise to the stresses and strains in the education system that many parents lament. Parents, teachers, principals and students themselves – as well as 'the system' – are all culpable, as Neo makes clear in his film. Indeed, I could not help but wonder, when reading the earlier reports of how more neighbourhood schools had managed to chalk up impressive gains in the number of students who scored well in the O-levels last year, just how this feat was achieved.

'Hot-housing' – or extra coaching for the students deemed to need it – was said to have played a part, according to the principals interviewed. Now, that is well and good, and the teachers and principals who put in the extra effort to help these students deserve to be commended. But it must be asked if there were not students who were pushed beyond their natural capacities – the proverbial 1600 cc engines being revved at 2000 cc levels – in the schools' quest to deliver such shining results. I hope not.

Talk to parents and you will hear many troubling anecdotes about schools where principals are driven by the need to produce top results to impress their bosses. The upshot of this is that some students get 'hot-housed'. Others are forced to drop subjects they like, such as literature, to pursue those that might be easier to score better grades in. This way, they will not pull the school's ranking down. Granted, some of these accounts might be embellished or even apocryphal. But speak to enough parents and you will get a sense of the high level of angst over such stresses in schools, sufficient to suggest that these concerns are not simply the stuff of a Jack Neo movie.

Pay attention. These concerns should be addressed, especially in this day and age, with all the emphasis on developing creative thinking, independent minds and an entrepreneurial spirit to ensure that our youth will thrive in the new global knowledge economy. It needs to be asked: Is taking on extra subjects and doggedly pursuing more and more A's the best way for students to prepare themselves for the jobs of the future? Would spending less time on their books give them more time to think, explore, experiment and even dream? As our students chalk up ever more impressive records in the number of A's they score, are they growing up with independent minds and with sufficient street smarts to fend for themselves, cook a meal, change a light bulb, play a sport and manage their health, or survive in a student hostel without a maid?

To be sure, this national obsession with academic grades and doing better than the Tans is deeply ingrained. I recall covering a speech in May 1997 by Lee Hsien Loong in which he highlighted the issue when he addressed teachers and principals. To make his point, he quoted from a speech by Dr Goh Keng Swee in which the one-time deputy prime minister and education minister had lamented Singaporeans' obsession with examinations. This had led to creative imagination, character and moral values being neglected, said Dr Goh.

This view was expressed in 1967, 30 years before the 1997 event, noted Mr Lee. But little had changed in the Singapore education system since then, he added. In fact, the situation seemed to have become worse, with students taking more and more subjects and having more homework. 'Already, my kids do more homework than I ever did – or at least they are supposed to do more than I have ever done – which I think is not quite necessary,' he said, drawing nods of approval from the teachers in the hall. Five years on, the situation remains. In fact, I would wager that more students these days are doing even more – not less – subjects and schoolwork, egged on by teachers and parents in the relentless race to stay ahead.

You will hear the same refrain from parents: What can I do? Everyone else is doing it. How can I hold my child back and dampen his prospects?

Clearly, if things are to change and this cycle of 'A-grade inflation' – more students feeling pressured by the system to do more subjects and pushing themselves to ace them – is to be broken, then some form of action from the authorities will be needed. Should schools be told to discourage students from taking more than five or six subjects at A-levels and eight at O-levels? Should the system for appraising teachers and principals make clear to them – and everyone else for that matter – that those who lead schools that do well in the value-added rankings will be as well rewarded as those that shine at mass-producing four-A students? Should junior college and university admission criteria as well as the scholarship selection process be changed to signal to students, parents and teachers that being bright does not only mean scoring more A's in ever more subjects?

Recognising this, the government has announced plans to change the university admissions criteria next year to include project work, reasoning tests such as the Scholastic Assessment Test and co-curricular activities. This is a step in the right direction, but it does not go far enough. Adding SATs and project work on top of the A-level results simply loads more onto the students. Unless the new system is modified to send a clear signal to students that it does not pay for them to pile on more subjects and focus only on getting better grades, many will continue to do so, in the hope of giving themselves an edge in getting a prized scholarship or a place at a faculty of their choice.

Here's an idea: Consider only the grades for a limited number of subjects for university admission. Supplement these with interviews, during which a student's creativity and character might shine through.

Now, I can just hear Ministry of Education officials rushing to their computers to respond to this and defend the status quo. They might say: '*Ling peh kong* (Hokkien for 'your father says', to borrow that expression from Neo)! Singapore's school system is one of the best in the world. Each child is given a chance to learn at his own pace. Streaming and customisation of the curriculum are key components of this system, which has been ranked tops in international studies. The ministry's Desired Outcomes in Education stress not only academic achievements, but also inculcating in students a love for lifelong learning.'

No doubt they are right. But unless something is done to tweak the incentive system in schools, for students and teachers alike, the problem of 'A-grade inflation' will continue.

So here's an assignment for MOE officials: Find ways to remake the system to ensure that some years down the road, another top government leader will not have to quote Mr Lee having said years ago that the system was loading more on kids than was necessary, and lament that, alas, the problem has not got better, but become worse.

(First published 16 March 2002)

233

Singapore is a conservative society, shaped by an Asian sense of propriety and the need to keep up an appearance of having an Asian sense of propriety. But growing education and exposure to the world has led some Singaporeans to push for a relaxation of rules and restrictions, causing a backlash from the more conservative silent majority.

Censorship: Let's not kid ourselves

FORMER American education secretary Bill Bennett was recently caught with his pants down, so to speak. Well-known in America as an outspoken moralist and social conservative, he made a name for himself writing books with titles like *The Book Of Virtues* and *The Moral Compass*, and appeared on talk shows preaching the harm caused by 'unrestrained personal liberty'. Hardly the sort of man you would expect to have lost US$8 million (S$14 million) gambling at Las Vegas slot machines, sometimes squandering thousands of dollars in an evening. As the British magazine *The Economist* put it in a recent article, 'You don't need to be a recently retired Democratic president to wonder if there is something just a little bit hypocritical about a man making millions out of preaching virtue and then feeding the proceeds into slot machines.'

In some ways, Mr Bennett's fall from grace is a pity. For all his foibles, much of what he wrote made good sense. He had a gift for telling engaging stories, gathered from around the world, which contained morsels of age-old wisdom. Ironically, the tale of his undoing carries a few morals of its own.

When I first heard about his comeuppance, I was reminded of Singapore's powerful social conservative lobby, which speaks up vociferously to 'protect society's values' whenever the debate turns to relaxing censorship, freeing up space for the arts, or opening minds through the Internet. Among them are the so-called 'Shin Min brigade' of mostly Chinese-educated Singaporeans who rail against any relaxation of censorship rules, even while some of them rush surreptitiously to cinemas in Chinatown to catch the latest R(A) movie, clutching a copy of the racy evening daily. So powerful is this conservative lobby that government ministers had to modify the film classification system after the 1991 general elections, to mollify those who felt liberalisation had gone too far, or so the story goes.

Their influence continues to this day. Just this week, I received an e-mail message from an irate reader of this newspaper expressing shock and horror that a Remaking Singapore group had proposed allowing 'dirty art' in Singapore. He was referring to a call for an end to the freeze on official funding for forum theatre and performance art, imposed after the infamous snipping of pubic hair during such a performance in 1994. I gather that the latest Censorship Review Committee's plans to relax some censorship rules had to be tempered after feedback from some grassroots leaders that the proposals would not sit down well in the Housing Board heartlands.

Don't get me wrong. I am not in favour of a libertarian free-for-all approach when it comes to censorship. Communities, I believe, have a right to assert some social norms. But I have a rough-and-ready theory of social policy: Nature abhors a vacuum. When public policy gets too far ahead of – or behind – private realities, the void is inevitably filled by hypocrisy, deceit or repression.

Consider this example: An American friend living in Singapore once lamented to me that a VCD of the film *The End Of The Affair*, based on the book by English author Graham Greene, had been brutally cut. Now, Greene was no porn artist but a talented writer who often wove Catholic themes into his books. In his 1951 novel, he tells the story of a couple living in London during the Blitz whose lives are blighted by an illicit dalliance. Ironically, the beautifully crafted film version was rated R when it played in American cinemas, but the video of the film was given a Parental Guidance or PG rating in Singapore, my friend noted. It is hard to fathom the logic in this: Why are videos for private viewing in Singapore given a looser rating than films for mass screening in the United States? Something seems out of whack, until you realise that the video version has been badly snipped and spliced for mass consumption. Yet, given its theme and the seriousness with which it treats it, the video is hardly likely to appeal to a mass audience and would probably be bought by only a small group of mature viewers, who are left frustrated and fuming at the cuts.

It might be asked, why do even R(A) movies have to undergo annoying cuts, as if adults over 21 years might shrink at the sights and be waylaid by the themes? Why are niche programmes like *Sex and the City* not allowed (until recently) even on late-night cable television?

The Remaking Singapore Committee, of which I am a member, took up these issues and recently recommended that the rating system for films be extended to more areas and the rules relaxed. The old argument for the present system and standards is that Singapore's censorship regime is a social compromise between its vocal cosmopolitan elite and the conservative silent majority in the HDB heartlands. It might be asked if this compact needs to be reviewed and updated, as society here matures and becomes more exposed to the wider world. Indeed, in the age of the Internet, far more stimulating fare is readily available to those who crave it.

Besides, walk around HDB housing estates and you will come across racks of racy videos brazenly being hawked to ready and willing buyers. Of course, the fact that these are available does not make them right. But it does raise questions about what people consider acceptable in private, even if some feel a need to be seen speaking out against them in public. Behind the prim and proper image that is often portrayed of Singapore's HDB heartlands, there seems to me to be plenty of life, labour and love going on. The reports that appear in the press from time to time of lovers' triangles ending in murders and maiming is just one seedy symptom of this.

I also very much doubt if the old compromise of 'zoning' out R(A) films from the heartlands and restricting them to downtown areas is relevant anymore. It used to be said that parents feared that their children might be scandalised and tainted if they came across saucy billboards outside their neighbourhood cinemas. Yet, in these days of cineplexes, screaming billboards are nowhere to be found. So is the pretence that having an R(A) film screened only at the Plaza Singapura cineplex and not Yishun 10 – a 20-minute MRT ride away – really necessary? How does this protect society's morals? Who are we kidding, apart from ourselves? Would a rating system, set at the right age and taste levels and properly enforced, not suffice?

Eventually, of course, a judgment will have to be made about what is acceptable in society today. But equally, every time I hear a holier-than-thou speech about the need to 'protect society', I cannot help but wonder if it passes the Bennett test and squares with the reality on the ground.

In today's world, simply saying that something will not play in the HDB heartlands may no longer be enough. The old majority-rules, one-size-fits-all approach will have to be updated and applied in a more sophisticated and tolerant fashion, with more room for minority interests and pursuits, if Singapore is going to be a global cosmopolitan hub able to attract talent from around the world – as well as keep its own talent – to work and live here. Singapore need not be Las Vegas when it comes to issues of public taste and values, but it should make sufficient accommodation if it aspires to match the likes of London, Tokyo and New York.

(First published 5 July 2003)

There is nothing like being away from home to make you value it more. I discovered this during a sabbatical year I spent at Harvard University's John F. Kennedy School of Government in 2000. I loved Boston and especially the beautiful countryside around. But it also made me appreciate some of the less obvious aspects of Bedok Town, which was close to where I lived before heading to the United States.

From Boston to Bedok

THE STAR-Spangled Banner fluttered in the languid night as over 500,000 people, mostly American, cried out 'This land is your land... this land is my land', before going on to extol America the beautiful, from sea to shining sea. It was the Fourth of July, and I had gone where the sensible dread to tread. I joined the hundreds of thousands who braved the crowds for the annual outdoor concert by the Boston Symphony Orchestra to mark the 224th anniversary of America's much celebrated declaration of independence in 1776.

The crowd, from old Irish immigrants to newcomers from China to Cuba, from the legendarily uptight white Anglo-Saxon New Englanders to more bohemian gay couples embracing openly, had gathered at the waterside Hatch Memorial Shell along the Boston Esplanade for the annual jamboree. Some had arrived as early as 7 a.m. to stake out the best spots (you thought only Singaporeans were *kiasu*?) in the bring-your-own blankets and picnic affair.

It was an evening to remember, in more ways than one. From the appearance by Don McLean belting out his ever-popular *American Pie*, to the thunderous cannon that bellowed in sync with Tchaikovsky's

1812 overture, and the 25-minute fireworks display over the Boston skyline that closed the night's festivities with a celebratory bang. For the most part, the crowd was cheerful, even joyous. People crooned 'My country 'tis of thee, sweet land of liberty, of thee I sing' as if they really meant it.

It was not all sweetness and light. Time and time again, the heat – it was so hot that mobile showers were installed – seemed to get the better of the crowd, and the ugly side of gracious American society reared its head. Where I was standing, there were frequent altercations between groups of people, with those at the back objecting to those in front dancing, thereby obstructing their view. Not surprisingly, the disputes soon became a matter of whose rights were being infringed by whom, as is so often the case in the United States.

'You have no right to stand there and block us,' several cried.

'We were here earlier. If you want a view, you should have been here at 5 pm,' someone shot back.

'If you sat down, we too could see,' came the reply.

And so the voices bandied salvos back and forth. Poor Tchaikovsky did not stand a chance.

I moved on to another section of the crowd. When the scene was repeated over and again, I eventually gave up, and resigned myself to the fact that classical music is best not heard in the midst of an unruly mob. I began to long for the peace and quiet of home.

I WENT to Boston exactly a year ago, last July, to pursue a master's degree in public administration at Harvard University. I had looked forward to arriving at the city's Logan International Airport, and taking in the sights of the so-called capital of New England. My expectations had also been raised by the frequent rallying calls by the Republic's government leaders that Singapore should aim to become the 'Boston of the East'. This had made me keen to see the Boston of the West, and just what it was that Singaporeans were constantly being told to aspire to.

Arriving at Logan was therefore a bit of a shock. Flying in from Singapore's Changi Airport into Logan, you cannot help but feel that you have left a developed country for a developing one, not the other way round. The airport is in disarray, with construction work going on everywhere. Efforts to improve and extend it beyond its present single runway have been stalled by lobby groups, from those who object to the noise that more air traffic would bring, to others who want to limit further economic development. (There is even a pressure group led by affluent urbanites who want to restrict the number of skyscrapers in the city lest these spoil their view!) The drive from the airport took me through the infamous Big Dig, a multi-billion-dollar project that aims to create a network of underground tunnels to replace the ageing highway system. Work has been going on for years, causing traffic delays and diversions, which look set to continue for nobody knows how long.

Despite these drawbacks, Boston is a pretty and charming city. Its residents take pride in the fact that the population swells by about 25 per cent to under one million when the academic year begins in autumn each year, and students – many of whom are from out of town, other states and countries – come streaming in to take up much-sought-after places at one of its many universities, from Harvard and the Massachusetts Institute of Technology, to lesser known but nonetheless respected ones such as Boston and Brandeis universities.

Given its small population base, Boston lacks the buzz of its bigger, richer counterparts, such as New York, Los Angeles or even Chicago. By comparison, its nightlife, restaurants and arts scene are hardly anything to shout about. It does have the great Boston Symphony Orchestra, which was ruled over by maestro Seiji Ozawa for decades, but even so, the arrival of a top foreign orchestra is regarded as a special event, which music lovers flock to, quite unlike the routine occurrence it would be in major cities like London or New York. You can drive through the downtown area in under half an hour, provided you do not get caught in one of its traffic snarls. But perhaps what did most to confirm the city as a world-class wannabe were the incessant speeches by political and business leaders alike that Boston is 'truly a world-class city'. Few in New York, London or Paris feel any need to assert the self-evident.

WHAT is it then about this city that enables it to draw so much talent to its universities, as well as Route 128, the so-called Silicon Valley of the West? To be sure, it has a pretty setting, with the spectacular Charles River running through the heart of it. But its weather is fickle and dismal, with hot summers and harsh winters. Bostonians often say that if you dislike the weather at any particular time, just wait a minute, for it will change before you know it. But after several weeks of seemingly interminable days of biting winds and sunless skies, I resolved never to complain about the heat and sunshine in Singapore again.

Singapore, in contrast, is a far more cosmopolitan place, with a wider range of people, cultures and cuisines. Indeed, many a time I felt that going from Singapore to Boston, I had 'downgraded' from living in a big city to a provincial one, and wondered why we in Singapore should shortchange ourselves by seeking to be the Boston of the East. After all, the emerging arts scene here looks more promising by the day, and a night on the town is still relatively cheap. Tickets to a Boston Symphony concert cost anywhere from US$30 (S$52) to US$100 apiece, while an ice hockey game will set you back by at least US$30 to US$50. Then there is the parking, Boston's answer to the Certificate of Entitlement scheme. If cars are cheap, motorists have to endure traffic jams and face great difficulty finding a place to park. And parking in the downtown area will cost you the princely sum of US$8–10 an hour, offpeak.

So what is Boston's draw?

Put simply, it is the people. The city's openness to talent, from wherever they may be, as well as its tolerance for diversity and ideas, seems to be its main selling point. Live and let live is the order of the day. Because being American is more of an idea than a reality based on race or culture, everyone assumes you are American, unless proven otherwise. This makes it easy for foreigners to fit in and enjoy the good life, American-style, or whatever style suits them.

Feeding on itself, the clustering of universities and research institutes here creates a focal point for thinkers and researchers alike. For all the leaps made in communications and technology, proximity still matters greatly, it would seem.

The upshot of this is simple: while Singapore has many advantages over Boston – from its sunny (albeit humid!) climate, to its cultural diversity, to its location at the crossroads of the East and West, and even its bigger size and scale – if it is ever to become the Boston of the East, it will have to embrace the flow of people and ideas, and all that that entails. This will mean less homogeneity in values and ideas, and even less control over public discourse. To their credit, government leaders have been busy declaring that such mindset changes are necessary and inevitable if Singapore is to make the leap into being a global player. Now is the time to translate rhetoric into reality.

THE first flurries of snow began to fall as I arrived at the Philadelphia airport. Rain and sleet had left the city wet and dreary. Arriving at my hotel, located next to the University of Pennsylvania, I was greeted by familiar-sounding voices. A group of students emerged from the hotel restaurant. Must be Singaporeans, I thought.

Despite the cold, rain and snow, nearly 300 Singapore students had made their way from all over the United States to attend a Singapore seminar organised by the Public Service Commission and Contact Singapore. As one of the speakers at the session, I marvelled at the lengths to which the students and the organisers had gone to bring this group together. It was a good opportunity for these young talented people to meet, bond and, hopefully, stay rooted to Singapore.

The young scholarship holders I met struck me as restless and eager to reach out and grab the opportunities unleashed by the new economy. I met a couple of fresh-faced men who had quit school after a year or two in the United States to chase their dream of becoming dot.com millionaires. Others, less intrepid, were sticking it out, but also wondering if they should keep to the tried-and-tested route of signing up with a big multinational corporation or government-linked company, or strike out on their own. They seemed ready, able and willing to plug and play on the World Wide Web. Heading home to familiar old Singapore, while still the option of choice for most, was not always the most attractive proposition.

At our discussion the next day, the topics on the students' minds were familiar old chestnuts: government attempts to control public debate, the media and the general direction of people's lives, including whether they spoke Singlish, came up for robust criticism. It was an uphill battle trying to convince the students that the future lay in their hands, that it was up to them to make a difference and shape Singapore the way they wanted it to be. If they wanted more space for public debate, then it was up to them to make it, not wait for government-sanctioned initiatives. That, after all, was the spirit of the Singapore 21 vision.

Many, however, dismissed the Singapore 21 effort as little more than propaganda. Clearly, it was not cool and hip to be seen to be 'pro-Establishment'. Those who hit out at some government policy or other drew the heartiest response. There seemed to me to be a certain disconnect between these young scions of Singapore society – the privileged and educated crème de la crème, on whom the country had placed its hopes for the future – and some of the fundamental tenets on which the society has thrived. All talk of Singapore's vulnerabilities, constraints, and why it sometimes needed to do things differently was met with stoic silence, perhaps even a touch of impatience. Having been there and done that, these young minds seemed inclined to move on. Yet, can these be wished away by so much insouciance and indifference?

AS THE F-16 jets thundered overhead, in a formation resembling the stars and crescent of the national flag, the excited crowd waved their red and white flags enthusiastically. The family of five beside me on the Padang for the National Day Parade had come from Bedok to catch the excitement of the big bash for Singapore's 35th birthday. I was glad to meet them, not least since they disclosed that many of my favourite shops and hawker stalls in Bedok, a short drive from where I used to live, were still around and thriving. Like many others in the crowd, my Bedok friends cried out when comedian Phua Chu Kang made his entrance in an NTUC cab, and they readily did the Padang wave, beating their drums and flashing their lights, all on cue. Having spent a year in a country where the race issue seethes under the surface – despite the progress that has been made in bridging the white-black divide, there were streets in the Cambridge suburbs that were all-black, tucked away from the all-white, middle-class American dream homes – I was happy to hear Chinese schoolboys and girls singing Tamil and Malay songs, and vice versa.

'This is home, truly,' rang out the voice of Dick Lee. As the crowds sang along, I felt glad to be back. For all the familiar old gripes about the lack of space, the heat, the costly cars and houses, the never-ending problems with neighbouring countries, the mindless killer litter, the mobile phones ringing in concert halls, the babies crying in cinemas, the angst over bond-breakers and even the constant haranguing by some politicians ever so quick to shoot the messenger, this was, in the end, home.

(Adapted from a piece first published on 8 August 2001)

Conclusion:
Is Singapore finished?

SINGAPORE is finished, done for, *habis, kaput!* This view, asserted with varying degrees of conviction, has been heard increasingly in recent years, from those at dinner parties to the chatter among the coffee-shop crowds. The economic boom years are over, as competition hots up from China and India. The joys of a tight labour market, with wage rises and big bonuses, and plentiful job offers for workers to choose from, are gone and never coming back. The ever-rising property market, which fuelled a once relentless drive to 'upgrade', cashing in on one's home for a bigger, better one, and pocketing the difference, is something that today's younger generation can only dream about, as they watch choice homes moving further beyond their reach. When politicians, who once pledged 'more good years', start telling voters that perhaps they might be better off chasing other, non-material, dreams, you know that times must really be tough.

So the talk in Singapore goes, especially at the height of the doom-and-gloom days of 2003, when Singapore was hit by a 'perfect storm' of woes – an economic downturn, a Sars outbreak, and US-led war in the Middle East.

Somehow, I just don't buy it.

The 'Singapore is finished' crowd was everywhere in the 1960s, when Singapore was thrown out of Malaysia and forced to cast about on its own for survival. It sprang up again when news broke of British plans to withdraw their forces from Singapore. It returned in the 1980s when a bitter recession struck, only to disappear in the boom times of the 1990s. From mid-2000, amid tough economic times, it once again became fashionable to doubt our prospects for survival.

To be sure, the naysayers are on firm ground when they point to the economic, social and political challenges ahead. China, India,

Malaysia and Thailand are fast rising and will pose a serious economic challenge to Singapore. Rapid technological change could also erode Singapore's competitive edge in any number of presently unfathomable ways. When, for example, Singapore Airlines began flying nonstop to Los Angeles this year using the latest long-haul planes, the excitement over this was surely tinged with a sober awareness that other airlines were also busy launching flights from Dubai to Sydney, bypassing Singapore. Overnight, the hub status that Singapore has built up for Changi Airport could disappear if technological changes lead to people changing the way they wish to travel, unless Changi finds new ways to entice them here.

But this, to my mind, in no way means that Singapore is finished. What it does mean is that Singapore's struggle, of continually striving to make itself relevant to the rest of the world, to stay ahead strategically and economically, will never quite be finished. Being small, vulnerable and dependent on trade to make a living, it will always have to find ways to overcome its inherent limits and exploit its strengths to make its way in the world. It has done so in the past, against the odds and contrary to the predictions of all the naysayers. Whether it can do so in the future depends on the wits and will of its people to continue making the effort to survive and thrive.

If we decide that the challenges are just too daunting, that the collective effort is just too much of a strain, that the pragmatism and nimbleness for which we have become famous are just too much of a price to pay to overcome our island state's inherent limitations, then Singapore's days might well be numbered. If Singaporeans forget how we overcame our past privations, take liberties with ourselves, and allow a younger generation to grow up believing that theirs is naturally an affluent, developed society as a matter of right, rather than by sheer dint of the grit and hard work of their forebears, then Singapore might really be finished.

But I just don't think it's going to happen anytime soon.

Call me an optimist, but having seen how Singaporeans have responded to a crisis time and again gives me a deep, abiding sense of confidence that we will be able to pull through in the future as well. The odds of our doing so rise each time we overcome one obstacle or another, whether it is an economic downturn, a Sars outbreak, or just a tricky period of political transition. In the process, over the years, Singaporeans have built up resources – in both financial and political capital – to help see us through difficult times down the road.

NO DOUBT many of the issues that have been discussed in the preceding pages will remain and recur in new guises in the years ahead, just as surely as new challenges will arise. For a long time to come, Singaporeans will have to grapple with ethnic differences, economic and strategic vulnerability, the stresses and strains that come from needing to put in that extra to give ourselves an edge. These will not change.

But nor, I think, will the derring-do and can-do spirit that has become a hallmark of Singaporeans over the years be easily extinguished. If Singaporeans can keep that alive and pass it on to a new generation, our place in the world might continue to be assured. How to do that is, to my mind, our biggest challenge for the future – not just for the government, but also for you and me. The work to keep Singapore going will never be finished.

INDEX